THE POCKET GUIDE TO
TROUT &
SALMON
F L I E S

COMPILED BY JOHN BUCKLAND

M I T C H E L L   •   B E A Z L E Y

The Pocket Guide to Trout & Salmon Flies

Edited and designed by Mitchell Beazley International Ltd
Artists House 14–15 Manette Street London W1V 5LB

Editors   Alan Folly and Elizabeth Pichon
Art Editor Mike Brown
Production Androulla Pavlou

Photographs by Mike Dunning
Artwork by Charles Jardine

© Mitchell Beazley Publishers 1986
Artwork © Mitchell Beazley Publishers 1986
Photographs © Mitchell Beazley Publishers 1986
All Rights Reserved

For their invaluable assistance in the compilation
of this book grateful acknowledgement is made to
The Orvis Company Inc, Vermont, U.S.A. and to
John Russell of Orvis U.K., Stockbridge, Hants.
Special thanks are due to Unwin & Sons Ltd of
Nandi Hills, Kenya, in association with FMF Tackle Ltd,
Reigate, Surrey, who researched and tied the flies
illustrated in the text.

ISBN 0 85533 609 9

The compiler and the publishers will be grateful for any
information which will assist them in keeping future
editions up to date.
Although all reasonable care has been taken in the
preparation of this book, neither the publishers nor the
compiler can accept any liability for any consequences
arising from the use of, or the information contained
herein.

Typeset by Servis Filmsetting Ltd, Manchester
Reproduction by Electra Graphic Systems Ltd, London
Printed in Hong Kong by Mandarin Offset Marketing (HK) Ltd.

CONTENTS

AUTHOR'S INTRODUCTION

In what seems to have been a lifetime spent in sporting journalism, I have had an unparalleled opportunity for travel. Yet this travelling habit originated well before I started and most of it has been for just one reason: to fish.

In the deep pine-forested ravines of Transylvania, where much of the talk, admittedly in Bulgarian, was of marauding wolf and bear; in New Zealand where the pumice rocks floated, glow worms lit the path down to the river and yellow-eyed goats glared at us suspiciously across the water; in both places my reason for being there was the trout!

As a youthful nineteen year-old I worked in a lumber mill in the extreme northeast of the United States. Every weekend I was out by plane or car and square-stern canoe in pursuit of char or landlocked salmon as the seasons permitted. In all this travelling in search of game fish, I had no overall guide to ease the way; I relied on snippets of local advice or, often as not, simple trial and error. No one was then producing anything like this small but information-packed guide.

In it I have attempted to present a logically organized illustrated selection of game fishing flies which truly represent the patterns that have proved their success through their popularity – flies which are used in every kind of water in all the game fishing countries of the world. It does not set out to be a reference for fly tiers, though I know many will find it useful as such. Nor have I tried to rationalize hook styles and sizes. Hook sizes vary hugely, not just between countries but between suppliers.

Fishermen who cross boundaries and travel long distances to fish are frustrated by this lack of consistency, but representation of the flies at the size most commonly used will, I hope, prove the most useful way of overcoming the problem. If individual patterns are tied in a wide variety of sizes I have indicated this in the captions. There are many excellent books on fly tying and there are many more superb books on fly fishing in every sort of situation. This book is primarily an identification guide to the fly patterns themselves – what they look like, where they come from, what they are used for.

Both the Publishers and I have been fortunate in the encouragement and advice we have received in its preparation. In particular the American-based fishing tackle company, Orvis, has drawn unstintingly on its experience trading worldwide. Throughout Unwin's and FMF Tackle Ltd have also been unreservedly helpful, and indeed have made the whole project possible by searching through their order books for the past ten years to produce the most consistently demanded and accepted fly patterns in use in all the game fish countries in the world. These are the patterns illustrated in the pages that follow.

For these companies and for me it has been quite an adventure finalizing the selection and then establishing the best format for a really practical and useful easy-reference guide. Of course it is possible that the reader will find some personal favourite neglected or missing from these pages, but overall there is a vast range of representative flies in each class, constituting really helpful guidance for all fly fishermen.

Though the English-speaking countries have produced a wider range of fishing literature than all the others put together, and influences from Britain and America permeate fishing theory and practice worldwide, local advice and experience are always well worth seeking and considering. Sometimes this is either not available or is limited, but

where it is, I have been happy to incorporate it here. In particular, the layout adopted for the colour illustrations which form the core of the book, allows comparison of points of style and similarity of flies from all over the world. This is a much more practical – and helpful – approach than an alphabetical or national set of listings could be.

I feel fortunate in being asked to compile this guide. In the course of many fishing trips around the globe, I have received innumerable kindnesses and much generosity. If this little book proves its value to fly fishermen everywhere, as I feel sure it will, then I feel I go some way to repaying this debt of gratitude.

JOHN BUCKLAND

H O W   T O   U S E
T H I S   B O O K

The illustrations are grouped in four main sections: *trout*; *sea-trout and steelhead*; *salmon* and *other game fish*. Each of these sections is sub-divided into *wet* and *dry* or, in the case of *other game fish*, *saltwater* or *freshwater*.

Each section is identified by a colour tab at the edge of the page, and the tone of colour then subdivides each section.

The index is alphabetical, giving the page number for the illustration of the named fly, together with the page number of any reference in these introductory pages or captions.

The flies have been arranged on the basis of colour, the most easily apparent element of similarity. The merit of this is that the fly fisher can then easily recognize the pattern, allowing him to match it to an insect he has seen the fish take, or to a tying recommended to him.

An angler visiting an unfamiliar water will see at a glance from these pages whether he needs to hurry to the nearest tackle shop or whether the flies he is carrying in his fly box are likely to provide good sport. Equally, knowing what sort of flies he will be likely to use when abroad, he can consult this book and then stock up with the nearest equivalents while still at home. Fly tiers may also discover styles and techniques which they can adopt or adapt into their own tyings. Although similar ideas on fly tying often occur simultaneously in many countries, theories and practices do differ, and just as innovations from Europe in the early 1900s certainly enhanced American fly fishing, so new trends can still be profited from internationally. A few historical patterns are shown in the photographs, but the main selection of flies is based on proven best sellers from patterns all over the world.

Each fly has been assigned to its particular section because (a) it was designed to catch a specific type/types of fish, and (b) by general practice it is used most often to catch those fish. That is not to say that flies in other sections will not catch a wide variety of game fish. Many sea-trout have been caught on salmon flies, and many salmon have been caught when sea-trout were the intended quarry.

Since the practices and the traditions of fly fishing have also been transferred to other forms of fishing (particularly saltwater fly rodding), the final section of this book contains illustrations of patterns for species which because of their valued qualities may also be called or treated as game fish, though they are not of the salmon or trout family.

No doubt some fishermen will decry the absence of their favourite pattern, or scorn the inclusion of another, but the guiding rule in making the selection for the illustrations has been to use the patterns and sizes which have proved their efficacy in fishing countries all over the world.

A word of caution: the flies illustrated here are tied on a variety of hook styles. Some flies have additional weight built into and under the dressing. Local rules, laws and regulations may, however, prohibit the use of double or treble hooks, or weighted nymphs. Don't run foul of such rules: remember that the dressings and profiles of the flies can also be achieved on hook forms which do comply with local rules, with little loss, if any, in their efficiency.

Naming and selection

"The brown fly" on its own just does not contain enough information, neither does "No. 3". What has evolved in the naming of flies, however, is a gradual standardization of names and dressings. If the original, exact, dressing for a Jock Scott (a salmon fly) is no longer possible, any change which retains the general concept should be called a Jock Scott variation. However, the modern versions of this ancient pattern are now easily recognizable and the variation is therefore no longer remarked.

Where it is useful, some early tyings are included in the illustrations, together with the modern interpretations, but most of the flies illustrated are as demanded by the fishing public from their suppliers or are part of general fly tying repertoires. Some amateur tiers' work is of such merit that their private experiments have subsequently become public property adopted by the trade and often such a pattern is prefixed by their name. But many patterns devised by keen amateurs will not feature in this book; their reputation is not sufficiently widespread, and their nomenclature unstandardized. This can mean that highly localized fly patterns, with a small and faithful following, may also not be listed. Nevertheless some, even if restricted, examples of modern fly tying have been included.

Definitions

There are some inescapable problems. In common usage the name of an insect and its corresponding imitation may be identical: for example, Olive Dun, the artificial pattern which may be tied in a number of styles, and olive dun, the sub-imago stage of the insect *Baetis*. The Dark Hendrickson likewise is both the insect and the pattern dressed to imitate it. A Greenwell's Glory, however, is a pattern and not an insect, so it is a mark of extreme naivety in Britain to talk of "a good hatch of Greenwells" (unless the speaker is a humorist). However, in North America many fly patterns were devised before Latin names had been established for the natural insects they imitated. As a result, Americans often call their upwings by the names of the corresponding artificials.

The word mayfly is also ambiguous. In Britain it is the definitive term for just one group of upwing flies. Elsewhere it refers to upwing flies in general. In some locales the stonefly is called a mayfly. What is called a sedge fly in many areas is called a shad fly in others, yet the patterns of artificial fly designed for catching shad are also loosely termed shad flies! Where confusion is likely to arise, the caption notes will help.

References to wing can also be confusing. Each of the following could be meant: the wing of a natural insect; the wing as part of the artificial fly imitating the wing of the natural; the wing of an artificial fly which imitates a fish by means of a bundle of hair or whole feathers tied at the top of the hook; and the wing of a bird from which suitable fly tying materials are taken. Again, the captions will clarify.

GAME FISH

Though other species of fish are caught on the fly, game fish are the primary quarry because of their sporting qualities, their appearance and their value as eating.

When referring to them we are concerned with three main branches of one family grouping:

1. The Atlantic salmon, and the trout in various species
2. The chars
3. The graylings

Often there is a resident (or landlocked) form, and a migratory (or anadromous) form which leaves freshwater for rich feeding in the sea, and then returns to the freshwater (whence it came) to spawn.

In terms of fly fishing most of the information which follows refers specifically to the resident brown trout, but it applies equally to the other resident species, because their freshwater habitats and requirements are very similar.

Atlantic salmon

The salmon is more widespread and numerous in its migratory form that in its landlocked, so for much of the lifestyle of the landlocked fish the details relating to trout should be read.

In general, migratory fish either do not feed in freshwater, do not feed regularly in freshwater, or have no need to feed in freshwater, having stored in their tissues all the richness of abundant sea food required for spawning. The flies for migratory fish, therefore, are rarely imitative; they are usually fancy or attractor, intended to arouse the curiosity of the fish, or to stimulate its feeding or predatory instincts.

Fly fishing can basically be divided into two branches – wet fly with flies presented below the surface film; and dry fly with the presentation in or on the surface. Both dry and wet flies may be imitation/deceivers of a food form or attractor/lures which give an illusion of something that the fish wants.

About 90 percent of fish diet is taken below the surface, so perhaps more wet fly patterns exist than dry fly patterns. However the enjoyment of the stalk of fish which can be seen feeding at the surface, and often the extra delicacy and finesse necessary to catch them has made dry fly fishing the height of enjoyment for many anglers. The fish tend to be extremely selective, so a large number of patterns have been devised, many of them alternative forms to imitate one particular insect in each of its development stages.

T R O U T

Brown trout *(Salmo trutta)*

This is the native trout of Europe, introduced widely into countries in both the northern and southern hemispheres where it has thrived. Because it has always been a classic quarry of the fly fisher, its lore went with it to its adopted countries. For example, the traditions it brought with it to America in 1883 saw the start of new angling techniques on both the eastern and western seaboards.

The brown trout is equally at home in streams, rivers and stillwaters (lakes or reservoirs) provided the water is pure enough and has sufficient oxygen. In general it is a light golden brown in colour with liberal blackish or brownish spotting on back and sides. Sometimes these spots are entirely red. It possesses a chameleon-like capacity to camouflage itself against its surroundings, the dark heavily spotted fish being found in deep dark areas, while the lighter fish may be expected in clearer water and against lighter backgrounds. The tail is rarely spotted compared with that of the rainbow trout.

Growth and maximum size is dependent on the availability of food. Fish over 10lb (4.5kg) are real trophies though the maximum is in the region of 40lb (18kg). Two-pounders and upwards (1kg) are all good fish.

It is the most fastidious of the trout family; selection of the correct pattern to catch it is more critical than for the freer taking char and rainbows.

Brown trout

The brown trout has been successfully introduced into Tasmania, mainland Australia, New Zealand, South Africa and other African countries, as well as North and South America. Where feed has been especially rich specimen fish have regularly reached enormous weights. This was particularly true of the early years in New Zealand and Argentina.

Its migratory form, the sea trout, is also classified as *Salmo trutta*. When newly arrived from saltwater it is more silvery than the resident brown trout, but as it darkens with spawning maturity, the differences between the two are less easy to distinguish.

9

Rainbow trout *(Salmo gairdneri)*

The rainbow trout is now almost as widespread as the brown, acclimatizing readily in areas where it is not a native, provided the water is sufficiently pure and does not reach temperatures which are critical to its survival. It has a wider temperature tolerance than brown trout. The general classification is *Salmo gairdneri* which includes its migratory form, the steelhead.

The fish is more silvery than the brown trout, generously freckled with black spots, with tail and fins markedly spotted. The magenta blaze along the flanks, giving the fish the name rainbow, is another distinguishing feature, though there is wide variation in colouring and marking dependent on locality. This trout is more free-rising than the brown, and the imitative range of fly patterns has never been as necessary as the attractors.

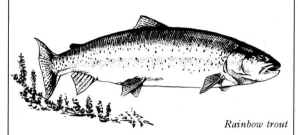

Rainbow trout

This willingness to strike at a fly has led to the fish's immense popularity with fly fishers all over the world. It is also easy to rear, and in waters which are heavily fished, it is very suitable for stocking. Because of its ease of rearing, this is a popular table fish, farmed specifically for the food trade.

Probably the finest examples of rainbows are the wild fish found in Alaska – immensely strong and acrobatic. When hooked they are a real sporting test of a fisherman. The rainbow's growth rate is more rapid than that of the brown trout, and it lives less long; however a fish of over 50lb (22.5kg) has been recorded. Good fish weigh over 2lb (1kg), and any wild fish of 10lb (4.5kg) upwards constitutes a trophy.

Cut-throat trout *(Salmo clarki)*

This is the only other important true trout. The cut-throat earns its name from a vivid scarlet slash around the bottom of the gill cover and lower jaw. Unfortunately this fish hybridizes easily with rainbows, and it may be difficult to distinguish between them. Basically the cut-throat is a silver fish with black spotting continued into the fins and tail. Its tail is square-ended while that of the rainbow is somewhat rounded in its top and bottom lobes.

Its natural range is on the western coast of America; in its wilder habitats it can be a shy and choosy feeder, but in general it rates second class to the more vigorous rainbow, steelhead and brown trout, even the larger sea-going forms lacking angling appeal.

C H A R

This is a group in which some of the members are confusingly – and inaccurately – called "trout". Char, however, are much more finely scaled, smell quite different out of the water and have a different arrangement of teeth. Their markings also differ: a white leading edge to fins and orange or red spots on a darker (olive) background are clues to identification.

Arctic char *(Salvelinus alpinus)*

In its migratory form this fish can weigh up to 25lb (11kg), but 2–3lb (1–1.5kg) are the expected sizes. They will strike at brightly coloured attractor flies, fished with angler-induced movement, and fished deep. In freshwater they rapidly lose interest in taking, though occasionally they will take a dry fly. The patterns, wet or dry, are not as important as finding the fish in a mood to take.

The resident char, which are smaller, are widespread in the northern hemisphere, but not in vast numbers. They are a shoaling fish and in Britain normally remain in the depths of the deeper stillwaters and lochs though they occasionally come to the surface and will accept flies. As the males reach spawning readiness they lose their silvery appearance, their flanks turn scarlet, and their markings deepen in intensity, the white edge to the fins becoming particularly apparent. The Dolly Varden *(Salvelinus alpinus malma)* is also grouped within the arctic char family. It too has a sea-going form, but though a 32-pounder (14.5kg) has been recorded it is less favoured as a sporting fish than the more active and vigorous steelhead and rainbow trout.

Brook trout *(Salvelinus fontinalis)*

This is another char. In the early days of American fly fishing it gave rise to the multiplicity of fancy wet attractor patterns, but the brook trout declined in numbers with the onset of denser human populations combined with agriculture and forestry operations extending over the eastern American seaboard. The back of the fish carries vermiculations in addition to spotting, and its fins are patterned, distinguishing it from the arctic char forms.

The 1916 record of 14lb 8 oz (6.5kg) is soon likely to be broken in Argentina where the brook trout is now flourish-

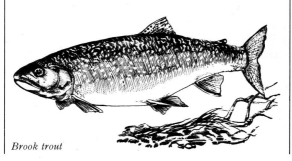

Brook trout

ing. More normal fish weigh around 1lb (.5kg) and remark-
ably sea-going examples do not attain greater weight than
the resident fish.

A prime requirement of this fish is cold, pure water.

Lake trout *(Salvelinus namaycush)*
The third important char is also called the togue, Great
Lakes trout, gray trout or mackinaw; it is, however, still a
char. Commercial fishing has brought fish of over 100lb
(45kg) to the surface, but the fly fisher is unlikely to catch a
fish over 20lb (9kg), as the larger ones hug the depths. The
deeply forked tail and dark greyish-brown back, shading to
a lighter belly, flecked with small pale spots, distinguishes it
from the other chars, as does its habit of fighting deep.

In general, it responds better to spun lures and trolling
than fly fishing, but fish are taken regularly on streamers,
often in the course of landlocked salmon fishing.

G R A Y L I N G

Grayling are easily distinguished from the other game fish:
they have an immense dorsal fin with twice the number of
supporting rays, an underslung mouth with few apparent
teeth, and a sharply forked tail. Taken together, these
features make grayling unmistakeable. They are not as
widely distributed or as numerous as trout.

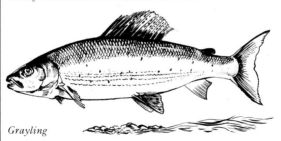

Grayling

The grayling is a spring spawning species (unlike trout
which spawn in late autumn and early winter), a factor that
extends the fly fishing season in many countries. Grayling
are also prepared to feed in lower water temperatures when
other game fish are lethargic.

The arctic form *Thymallus arcticus* is the heaviest with 3-
and 4-pounders (1.5–2kg) a reasonable expectation. Lapland and North America both offer this fish. Smaller fish are
the Montana grayling and the European *Thymallus
thymallus* of which the latter fish averages under 1lb (.5kg)
with any example over 2lb (1kg) exceptional. Delicacy is the
keynote to catching them. Flies are smaller: casting and
presentation have to be extremely accurate and as grayling
are a shoal fish, the fright of one can spread alarm to the rest.
Many of the trout patterns take grayling, as do specific
grayling patterns take trout.

On the European continent grayling are more highly
esteemed than elsewhere.

S A L M O N

Migratory Atlantic salmon *(Salmo salar)*

"Doubtless had God Almightly so minded he would have made a more perfect fish, but it is certain he never did." It is a sad fact that these magnificent fish are diminishing in numbers. Many of the rivers that hold them are becoming too polluted to support them any longer, and commercial sea fishing and poaching have both taken an immense toll.

Yet for many fishermen they are still the greatest of the freshwater game fish, with their essential swiftness, power and mystery. The salmon eggs hatch into small fry which spend their first two or three years behaving very much like young trout, feeding and putting on weight and size until they reach about 6–9in (15–23cm) long. They then lose their trout-like appearance, don a silver coat and, as smolts, drop down river to the sea. The sea then provides rich feeding, and in due course the salmon return to their home freshwaters in which they, in turn, will spawn. Those fish which return after only one year at sea are termed grilse, and the sort of weight they reach varies between 3lb and 9lb (1.5–4kg). Fish which spend two or more years feeding at sea range from about 5lb (2.25kg) to real monsters of 30–50lb (13.5–22.5kg). World-wide an average salmon weighs about 10lb (4.5kg).

When the urge to return to their home river is on them, they head back to that river's estuary and await the necessary flow of water, for they travel upstream more readily in a full rather than a drought-struck river. They have now stopped feeding, their flesh is rich in energy-giving oils and their spawn is ripening. The mystery and the challenge are now apparent: the fish have no need to feed, their digestive systems have atrophied, yet the fly or bait of the angler is sometimes accepted, why we do not know.

It is only in relatively recent years that salmon has been fished for sport; previously their value was solely commercial and realised in netting or fish traps. The early fly fishermen believed that as salmon were found in rivers, they should be treated like trout – larger trout lying in deeper stretches. Thus flies for salmon were initially larger scale versions of trout flies. However, this simple state of affairs did not last. With the increase in trade and the growth of the British Empire in the nineteenth century, the traders and colonizers brought home trophies from many far-off countries. The fly tiers and designers decided that such garish colours would add extra attraction to sombre and sober salmon flies, and from the middle to the end of the nineteenth century a rash of new and improved salmon fly patterns was offered by the trade to attract first of all the angler, and then the fish.

The fish would probably have continued taking the sombre patterns previously offered, but the fashion had changed: each river was now allocated its own list of special patterns, with a few general patterns for all rivers. A whole science built up, based on the very doubtful premise that the salmon could be taught to take particular patterns.

This then was the heyday of the art and craft of fly dressing. "The fly dresser finds room for the utmost nicety of calculation in arrangement and adaptation, as well as a field for the imagination in realizing symmetry, proportion, mobility and colour harmony''. Science would supersede chance! If salmon really did feed in the manner of trout, science might be necessary. One hundred years later we have no greater knowledge than the Victorians had, and we still catch these fish.

The most successful salmon fishers do, however, work to conventions: they obtain local knowledge where they can, and *size* and *pace* of fly, and *depth* at which the fly is fished, all are combined in an equation with *water colour, height of river, temperature* of air and of water. They then select from their fly box a fly which meets their requirements, and in which they place confidence. If they also happen to be in the right place at the right time, they catch fish. Science in this case translates to mean experience, and a good caster who presents his fly well will in aggregate catch more fish, though beginner's good luck is notorious!

For every 200 salmon caught on a wet fly, perhaps only one is caught on a dry fly. In British waters a floating trout fly, presented to trout, is occasionally taken by a salmon but relatively few fishermen go out with the intention of catching salmon on a dry fly. In North America some of the rivers are more shallow and more generously stocked with fish, particularly with rather competitive grilse. An appreciable rise in water temperature in the course of the day is regarded by some dry fly fishers as a necessity for success; Labrador and New Brunswick in particular provide these conditions, and sport there can be fast and furious, with better results than with standard wet flies. However, despite well-documented reports of success with a dry fly, it is the tried and tested wet salmon fly, so formalistic in its tradition, that is fished most.

A cynic has suggested that only the rivers where the salmon fishing rents are in the Rolls-Royce class are the ones where the traditional salmon flies work best! In lesser waters simpler styles and dressings are the fashion, based on their cheapness of manufacture. In fact the wheel has turned full circle – there is no proven need for the multi-hued complicated lines of past history, and simple mobile flies which take little time to tie and do not call for the feathers of endangered birds are quite as effective.

The naming of the patterns does have a practical reason – one fisherman can communicate succinctly with another. If only fly sizes could be communicated so easily!

Landlocked salmon *(Salmo salar sebago)*

These fish are Atlantic salmon which either cannot migrate to the sea or do not choose to. They occur naturally on the more northerly part of the eastern coast of North America and in Canada; they have also been introduced to South America and to New Zealand, and there is a small Scandinavian group. The fish resemble the more usual migratory salmon, but tend to be more heavily spotted. They could be confused with silvery examples of brown trout, but are more coarsely scaled. When the feeder streams to the lakes warm up at the start of spring, the ice on the lakes at their inflow starts to melt and clear areas extend. Large streamer flies to imitate smelt, a small bait fish, are then used, either flycasting or trolling. The landlocks strike hard and give magnificent runs, with leap after leap until they are eventually subdued. Fish of about 2lb (1kg) upwards are the norm, with fish of over 4lb (2kg) becoming worthy of extra admiration, though the maximum weight observed is over 20lb (9kg).

Streamer patterns are not the only effective ones, however, and later in season standard wet and dry flies are used.

Pacific salmon (*Oncorhynchus*)

The term "salmon fishing" is normally applied to fishing for Atlantic salmon. This is not to deny the existence of the species of Pacific salmon so prolific off the western coast of North America. Two of these species, the chinook and the coho, have proved themselves fine sport fish, but a tradition of fly fishing and fly tying for them has never developed. Instead, the most effective lures for both are spoons, plugs and wobblers, or natural baitfish rigged with hooks, fished deep, often off shore or in tidal saltwater. However, the introduction of both species to the Great Lakes in 1967 has resulted in an increasing interest in fly fishing for them, either with existing or adapted streamer flies, with steelhead or with Atlantic salmon flies.

First in importance is the chinook (*Oncorhynchus tshawytscha*), also known as the king salmon – and as the tyee when its weight exceeds 30lb (13.5kg). The sport record is 92lb (42kg) and the largest known caught in nets 126lb (57kg). Introduced into the Southern Hemisphere, it has been neither a failure nor an outstanding success. In New Zealand, where it is known as the quinnat, the most usual method of fishing for it is spinning, fly fishing having consistently proved a waste of effort.

In its smaller sizes the chinook can be distinguished from the next most important Pacific salmon, the coho or silver salmon (*O. kisutch*) by the pale interior of its mouth, the coho having blackish gums. Although coho of over 30lb (13.5kg) have been taken, they average out at between 6–12lb (2.75–5.5kg). Hard fighters with a repertoire of acrobatics, they are popular with anglers. Coho are more ready to take a fly than chinook, though plugs, spinners and spoons account for most of those caught for sport.

In commercial, cannery, terms the pink salmon (*O. gorbuscha*) and the sockeye (*O. nerka nerka*) are the most valuable. The pink (also known as the humpback) runs at about 4lb (1.8kg) and the sockeye up to, though seldom exceeding, 7lb (3kg). Flies for both should be fished deep, but most fish are caught in tidal waters or just into freshwater with spinning and baitcasting rods.

The smallest of the Pacifics is the landlocked form of the sockeye, the kokanee (*O. nerka kennerlyi*). As it averages about 1lb (.5kg), with a record weight of 4lb (1.8kg), it requires only light tackle. Widely and successfully introduced in North America as a resident lake-dwelling gamefish, it has become a popular sport fish with a lifestyle typical of its adopted environment.

In fly fishing terms probably the least appealing of the Pacific species is the chum or dog salmon (*O. keta*). These fish do not have the attraction of great size, averaging 5–10lb (2.25–4.5kg), they run late in the season and utilize the lower reaches of the rivers for spawning.

WHAT FISH EAT

Many of the flies shown in the plates will relate either to the mayflies (upwinged flies), to the caddis or sedges, or to the chironomids or midges. At a number of stages in their lives these insects are vulnerable to feeding trout and are preyed on heavily.

The most obvious are the flies that are seen on the water in the daytime, particularly on slow-flowing clear rivers and lakes. Probably a disproportionate amount of time has been spent by entomologists and fly tiers concentrating on these species, and this intense study has led to a cult of dry fly fishing. Thus mayflies have become virtually synonymous with trout fly fishing, yet in some areas they do in fact form only a small part of what trout actually eat.

The sedges in their developing stages are also taken very keenly by trout, but only recently have really effective patterns been devised which benefit the fisherman.

A very large number of chironomids are found on the menu of trout which live in still waters. The haphazard approach to wet fly fishing on large open areas of water, with three flies, tail, middle dropper and bob, has largely passed, and intensive fishing with one fly, a larval or pupal imitation of a chironomid, has taken its place, with more consistent results.

Mayflies
These are the aquatic insects most readily recognized as being a staple diet of trout. Their delicate wavering flight and elegance at rest, with wings folded vertically like a butterfly, makes them a favourite insect of the fisherman.

Mayfly adult

Mayfly nymph

The stages in their development are: egg, small nymph which moults regularly as it grows, large nymph ready to hatch or emerge, immature winged insect called sub-adult, sub-imago or dun, and after one final moult the imago or spinner, the adult. In this final stage the exhausted dying insect spreads its wings flat, like an aeroplane, lying *in* rather than *on* the surface film. The stages for imitation are: large nymph, hatching nymph/emerging dun, dun and spinner. Life expectancy once the sub-imago stage is reached may be as little as a day to as long as three days.

The abundance of the various upwings in the rich clear alkaline waters of southern England gave rise to the development of dry fly fishing, with its cult of fishing the rise: waiting for fish to show, feeding at the surface. Then the exact imitation is selected and offered the fish. Brown trout was the normal quarry, and when these trout were intro-duced to America in 1883 dry fly fishing came too.

Slow clear waters give the fish plenty of time to examine the fisherman's offering, and if some aspect is not quite right, the fish does not take. The colour of the wings, the legs and the body of the insect must accord with what the fish expects, and the insect colour can differ, both among insects of the same sort (say blue-winged olive) and also depending on whether fresh-hatched or nearing moult to imago stage.

The bewildering multiplicity of patterns has arisen because of this, and because the trout can be so selective in what they eventually take. The translucency of the materials is deemed of great importance by some tiers, and this will differ in direct or reflected light. Sometimes the imitations presented may all be excellent, but the fisherman may not have spotted that the fish are choosing another species of upwing hatching at the same time. Mayflies do not frequent just the slow waters; they are found in both still waters and rushing torrents. Each form of mayfly will be adapted to its habitat; the nymphs of some will be crawlers, or darters, or swimmers. Colour, shape and size all need accurate copying, but there are generalized profiles and silhouettes, and if the natural movement can be simulated the pattern becomes less important. The mayfly, the British insect, biologically *Ephemera danica* or *E. vulgata*, has been given extra names, Green Drake, Grey Drake and Spent Gnat, and these names have also been applied to the larger American upwings, and to the flies which imitate them.

Caddis flies or sedges

Representatives of this family of insects are to be found in almost every type of fresh water habitat. The larval stage is swiftly recognizable because the grub builds itself a case or home in which it can protect its soft body, with its head and legs protruding. The case may be of sand, fine gravel or particles of vegetation, depending on the kind of caddis fly.

Imitations of the cased caddis are not very prolific, though this is an area of growth among contemporary fly tiers, particularly in America. These imitations are normally weighted, and the technique used is to drift them along the bottom of the river or stillwater.

The pupal stage is more easily imitated: the grub having pupated within its case, leaves the case behind and heads for the water surface. It is vulnerable on its way up and in the surface film.

Sedge pupa   *Sedge adult*

The adult, recognizable by its moth-like appearance, with wings folded back over the body in tent form and with long antennae, is particularly at risk at the stage of egg laying, returning to the water surface or diving through it to swim down to lay its eggs.

In the daytime the adult flies normally hide among the waterside plants, and they take wing as dusk deepens.

When the flies land on the water surface they struggle – a trigger to hungry trout. The dry fly imitation may float naturally or be given twitches to resemble the behaviour of the real insect. Precision of pattern in both pupal and adult imitations can be very important, especially if the fish are proving selectively preoccupied with one species.

Stoneflies

The adult stoneflies fold their wings horizontally over their backs. Some have two tails, some have two little tail stumps, but they cannot as adults be confused with upwinged flies. As nymphs, however, there are similarities, and they are also favoured as food by trout. Their preferred habitat is in streams and rivers with gravelly and stony bottoms. The insects are mostly dull browns, greens and yellows, and their dogged but poor flying ability distinguishes them from members of the sedge family who are altogether better aviators.

Stonefly nymph   *Stonefly adult*

Vulnerable stages are as larvae or nymphs and as adults in their egg laying phase, either swimming in the surface film or dipping down to release batches of eggs. An artificial stonefly is included in one of the earliest recorded lists of recommended fly dressings.

Dragonflies and damselflies

Insects as large as these which depend on an aquatic environment sooner or later find themselves victims of a trout's hunger. The nymphs make a juicy morsel well worth imitation and the adults, though strong fliers when hardened off, can fall helplessly on the water as they straighten and dry their wings after hatching. A good general nymph imitation might well tempt deep-feeding game fish, when there is little sign of their activity at the surface.

Damsel nymph

Chironomids

Although in the late nineteenth century fly tiers had casually observed that still water trout included the non-biting midges in their diet, the practical importance of these insects long escaped attention.

Midge
larva

Midge
pupa

Midge
adult

Chironomids are two-winged flies, with a wide distribution, and they come in many sizes from very small to medium large. Their body colours are also many and varied: orange, red, brown, olive, black, grey and green. They are particularly appreciated by trout in the larval and pupal stages and occasionally in the adult stage. The antennae are normally feathery; legs are long and weak, and the body usually extends beyond the wings which are translucent. The larvae are small and thus difficult to imitate; the pupal stage is the especially vulnerable stage, and artificials can be very successful when the trout are concentrating on the natural pupae.

The humped thorax and whitish head filaments are especially noticeable and feature in many of the better fly designs. Alternative names for the midges are Blue-and-Blacks, Duck Flies or Buzzers.

Terrestrials

This is the term commonly used for insects which are not ecologically aquatic insects at any stage in their development but occasionally find themselves on the water, and, shortly after, in the insides of the trout. Beetles and grasshoppers are obvious examples, as are caterpillars which have lost their footing, and various of the *Diptera* (two-winged flies) and ants.

Grasshopper

ARTIFICIAL FLIES

Development

A worm, prawn and shrimp are strong enough to have a hook threaded through them without breaking apart. Also it is possible to cast them considerable distances while still attached firmly on the hook. Only the largest insects, however, are big enough to be pierced securely by a hook, and even then they are too fragile for casting. The alternative, known for many years, has been to make imitations of those insects which would otherwise be suitable natural bait. Since flies in this category have wings, the artificial flies were often given wings, but the early patterns were not expected to float. Instead they were held out over water and then allowed to drift round in the flow, under the surface. This tradition of winging wet flies is still with us, though in fact most natural subaquatic insect life does not have wings. As tackle improved it became possible to cast further and control the imitation fly better. Upstream fishing became practical. Dry flies came into use, and at the turn of the nineteenth century two earnest schools of thought were in conflict. The purists believed that only fish which rose to insects on the surface should be fished for, and then only with an imitation which was an exact replica of the natural fly the fish was selecting. Trout and grayling were the pawns in this game, for although salmon fishing continued as wet fly fishing, many dry fly anglers saw wet fly fishing for trout (the other school) as something less than sporting despite its long tradition. During the first 40 years of this century, however, it was established that over half of the trout's feed is subaquatic. All the stages of their underwater feed were subsequently studied and classified, and the results have provided the fly tying concepts we follow today.

What a fish sees

Modern scientists are certain that fish do have colour perception. The whole structure of the fish's eye suggests it. What fly tiers try to achieve in their insect imitations is what the fish sees in both direct and reflected light. When the insect is between the fish and the light source the upwings, for example, transluce, and the wings of some of the *Diptera* iridesce. For both these aspects a method of imitation has to be found. Some materials such as wool and silk alter their colours when wet, or when treated with oil or other flotants, and how to make use of this property is part of the science of fly tying.

Some natural materials can also fluoresce, which normally dyed materials do not. Fluorescence can now be added to patterns by modern dyes, as can phosphorescence.

A possible explanation for the multi-hued wings of salmon flies is that somewhere in the medley of colour will be the one which the salmon sees and likes!

Colour is not the only important aspect of a fly. Fish also see shape and observe movement. An irresistible shape of the wrong tone or tint may well take a fish, and a movement indicative of life may override the considerations of wrong colour and wrong shape. The best flies combine on the points that appeal to the fishes' senses.

Dry flies

In both imitative or deceiver patterns the fisherman requires his fly to be or have:

1. The right size
2. The right "footprint" – the pressure points on the surface film which break up and distort the light
3. A high float (if necessary)
4. The right colour or colours
5. The right plane: the angle at which the fly rests on the water
6. The right shape and silhouette
7. The right movement: this may be induced by the angler, or be a function of some of the materials used
8. Visibility to fish and fisherman

If all these desiderata are achieved, no trout should ever refuse such an offering! However, there is the physical limitation of the hook which, though now available in various shapes for special imitative purposes, remains heavier than water, and with bend and barb undisguisable.

The other factors vary in importance, and a combination with priority on the most critical is usually the way a fly dresser sets about the design of a new pattern.

Calm clear slow water will float a delicate fly in great visibility. A rough tumbling stream will drown a delicate pattern, and even if it escapes drowning such an artificial fly will be extremely hard for an angler to observe. Since he must tighten the hook into the fish when it rises to the imitation, he will be fairly unsuccessful if he cannot see his fly clearly. So for him a riding fly of good visibility is a better fish catcher than a closer imitation of the appropriate natural insect which does not have these properties.

The other quality of dry fly fishing is presentation. If the best possible imitation is offered to the fish in an unnatural manner: too heavy a landing; tied to too thick a leader; drifting faster than the water on which it is floating; then the fish is less likely to take it, or may even be scared by it. Some dressings, then, have been devised to help the fly to alight gently and cock perfectly, presenting the correct plane. The incorporated materials which achieve this may often deviate from being an exact imitation.

Throughout the patterns illustrated in this book there are examples of dry fly design for migratory fish with large floaters which can scarcely be said to resemble nature, but offer attractive bulk or silhouette to the fish, and easy visibility to the angler.

Wet flies

These are the flies fished under the surface. The styles of dressing therefore differ from those of dry flies. Materials are generally softer to offer less surface tension and to break through the meniscus easily. They are also more absorbent.

The variation in styles and sizes is very wide: adult insect imitations, winged or unwinged, the immature aquatic insects in their various stages of development at diverse depths, fish imitations, and patterns which have no reference to natural organisms but which by colour or shape or a combination of these attract fish to take them.

In both deceiver and imitative patterns the requirements may be listed as follows:

1. The right size
2. The right colour or colours
3. The right shape or silhouette
4. The right plane, the angle at which the fly is presented to the fish's vision
5. The right movement; either angler induced or as a function of chosen materials
6. Appropriate weight

If the fly is representing a known trout food item a practical combination of the above will turn out a useful fly. However most salmon flies are wet flies, and with their noted lack of appetite salmon (as with other migratory fish) are less predictable than trout in their fly requirements. Fishermen will have theories and fly tiers will have theories, so fly design will be adapted to suit these theories with especial emphasis, possibly, on colour in one case or movement in another.

A fair rule of thumb is that small creatures are incapable of the greater speeds of larger creatures; therefore, wet flies should not be fished faster than the natural pace of organisms of like size. Some of the minnow imitations, in fact, can be more deadly when fished even slower than the natural bait fish. An ill or wounded minnow is more likely to provoke an attack from a trout than will its hale and hearty fellows. Colour is more clearly distinguishable near the surface than at maximum fishing depths with either turbidity or restricted light, and elements of fluorescence fade into insignificance only a few inches below the water surface. Patterns fished really deep should be based on careful attention to shape and movement, with less importance given to the subtleties of colour so important near the surface.

The need for presenting the fly at the correct angle to the fish needs a little further explanation. A minnow swims horizontally: a minnow imitation is more likely to be attractive, therefore, if it also swims horizontally. A midge pupa hangs vertically, so the tying and the presentation should both maintain this image. Attitude of fly will depend on whether it is fished upstream or down, and on a taut or on a slack line. The density of the line (which helps determine how deep it sinks) will also have its influence.

Wet fly fishing has a longer tradition than dry fly fishing; to some anglers it is less attractive because a wetfly is often presented at random rather than to a specific observed fish. More competent fishermen with equal facility fish wet or dry as rules permit and conditions demand, and this calls for judgment of what the fish are taking or are prepared to take below the surface, and at what depth.

Nymph fishing is a branch of wet fly fishing based initially on imitative patterns, and largely continuing in this vein, it has brought the dry fly purist approach to sunk fly fishing, with selectivity the keynote; i.e., the fly tier's choice of which particular fish to catch, and the singlemindedness of the fish in selecting one item at one stage of development only.

The materials

The first materials we know to have been used for tying flies were wool and the feathers from domestic poultry. From local animals more colours and textures were available: from mammals like otter, squirrel, weasel, stoat, water vole, hare, rabbit, fox, badger, dogs and cats came wools, hairs and dubbings of topcoat and undercoat; from birds like wild duck, grouse, partridge and pheasant came feathers to be bound round the hook shank to represent insect legs, or laid along the top of the hook to represent wings. Brighter colours came from carpets or domestic clothing and silks. Wires and tinsels were available from, for example, military uniforms!

The original flies were a mixture of attractors and flies which most certainly were attempts at imitation, and some of these early dressings still stand the test of time.

When world travel became more possible, and collections of wild animals and birds flourished, the brighter plumage of exotic tropical birds took the eye of fly dressers. Possibly the Irish started the trend towards brighter salmon flies, for the Scots spoke of the gaudy "Irish" patterns as useless in their rivers, but there is no doubt that they proliferated all over the salmon fishing world. The wheel has turned full circle now, with a return to almost mundane dressings that are easier and quicker to tie, which catch fish well, and which are cheaper. Also, the very birds which brought the glitter and glamour are now under threat as endangered species, so for conservation reasons their feathers may no longer be used. Synthetic materials – nylons, plastics, non-metallic tinsels, rubber (the list is endless) – together with bold dyes, easily applied, are now used in conjunction with the simple feathers and furs of long tradition.

Flies for other game fish

Although the practice of fly fishing has grown up around members of the salmon family, there are many other species which can be caught on the fly. These provide a challenge to the fisherman either because of the extreme difficulty of catching them, or because they are a real thrill to hook with their vigorous and exciting fights to get away.

In freshwater, flies have been designed for pike for many years, although live- and dead-baiting and spinning are generally recognized as better methods of capture.

The French rate the chub as fly fisher's quarry, although elsewhere the species is generally considered as a rather dull fish. The diminutive dace will also take a fly. For these coarse fish many of the patterns designated for trout in this guide can prove effective.

Tiger fish in Africa can be caught on a fly although usually a spinner is more effective. Silvery salmon flies with a short dressing on a long hook preserve the dressing from their razor-like teeth, and wire traces, not nylon leaders, are essential.

The bass of North America (and other countries to which they have been successfully introduced) will hit a fly, and some of the most ingenious dressings will be found in this section. Shad (sometimes called freshwater herring), can be fished for with a fly in their migratory runs up river, but this is normally of rather different style from game fish flies.

Where pure "strength for size" is involved it is the wide range of littoral saltwater fish that gives the fly rodder the ultimate thrill. The immensely swift bonefish, the acrobatic and often huge tarpon, the shy, elusive, strong permit, the vicious barracuda – the species are many – all will take a fly, even if this is not the easiest method of catching them. Size of fly and depth are more important than exact imitations. However, since shrimps, crabs and small fish form part of these fishes' diet, the flies selected should bear some resemblance to these creatures.

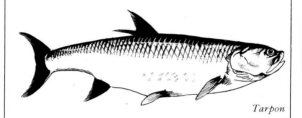

Tarpon

Care of flies

A certain amount of wear and tear must be expected – abrasion against waterside vegetation or grating against teeth in a bony jaw. It will be by luck rather than judgment if no major damage occurs in such circumstances, though well finished flies with whip finished heads, well varnished, are more robust than half-hitched and lightly varnished heads. The real enemy is corruption from moth and mist. Day-to-day storage of flies should not require any steps to prevent deterioration of wools, hairs and feathers, but long-term storage boxes should contain mothballs or modern anti-moth applications. Do give the fish credit for some sense of smell and taste. A heavily impregnated fly is not likely to be as attractive as an untainted fly, so give the well moth-proofed long storage flies a good airing before use.

Freshwater hooks rust, whether black enamelled or bronze lacquered. The result is fatal weakness in bend, barb and shank, and discolouration of the dressing. It makes sense, therefore, to carry a special receptacle for receiving used flies in the course of a day's fishing, in order that saturated flies are not returned to a box to soak its other, dry inhabitants. The receptacle can later be emptied to dry off the flies it contains. Once dry, these are returned to their normal fly boxes.

When a dressing has become distorted or crumpled, the easiest way to bring it back into good condition is to hold it briefly, by means of tweezers, in the spout of steam from a boiling kettle (tweezers avoid personal pain). When the fly is dry it can go back into the box.

The traditional fishing hat may seem an excellent receptable in which to store flies – but it is, in fact, one of the worst breeding grounds of rust. So are the sheepskin fly patches on fishing vests. Remember too that long-term exposure to bright sunlight fades both natural and dyed materials, so avoid this if you possibly can.

THE FLIES
IN COLOUR

All fly fishermen should find the information contained in the captions both specific and helpful. The following points should be noted when studying the illustrations:

Name: Most American, British and Commonwealth flies have standard names by which they are known all over the world. However, some modern tyings, particularly non-traditional salmon flies, do not yet have commonly accepted names and can therefore only be described in general terms.

In Continental Europe, flies are frequently left unnamed, being referred to only by the original manufacturer's catalogue number. When subsequently tied elsewhere, such flies usually retain their original numerical designation. This system can pose identification problems for the unwary.

Country: The country indicated will either be that of origin or where most widely used – not always the same.

Styles: There are many winging styles for wet flies, the majority being represented in the illustrations. Most can be applied to most of the flies shown. The fact that a pattern is illustrated in one style does not preclude it being tied in other styles. Dry fly styles are also numerous, the Adams being well-represented. Other styles like Hackle-less and Upside-down are also illustrated.

Of the wet deceiver patterns, many have a dry equivalent; similarly, many dry patterns can also be tied "wet". This always needs to be kept in mind. The inclusion of a fly in a specific section (eg *Trout*) does not necessarily mean that is its sole classification. On a heavier hook, or tied more densely, or with some other appropriate variation, it could, for example, become an accepted pattern for sea-trout or steelhead. Captions indicate the commoner examples of such possible variations.

Colours: Deceiver patterns use various materials in their natural colours. If dyed colours are employed, this will be indicated in the caption. Conversely, salmon patterns often incorporate dyed materials, and the captions then prefix any undyed materials with the word "natural".

Viewpoint: Spinners and parachute flies are photographed from above; other flies are shown either from the side or three-quarter view to illustrate better how they are tied and their style.

Size: In most cases, the flies are illustrated in an average pattern size. Where they have been tied smaller to fit the page, this is invariably indicated. Sizes for deceiver patterns relate directly to the sizes of the insects being imitated. Of the attractor patterns, size range is as variable as the tier or fisherman chooses. Salmon patterns vary from the very large – to be fished deep and slow in the big waters of the early and late season – to the diminutive for summer conditions. Overall, the illustrations provide a wide-ranging selection of normal size flies, with both the larger and smaller being practical in use.

Captions occasionally refer by name to individual fly originators or tiers. Nearly all of these have written excellent books which are well-worth seeking out.

1 Black Chenille – *UK*. Bob
Church pattern of 1970 for
early season reservoir trout.
Popularizes chenille as body
material.
2 Black Muddler – *USA/UK*.
Important variation on
Muddler Minnow. Also
White Muddler, Yellow
Muddler etc. The Muddler
head is sometimes natural in
colour, sometimes dyed.
3 Black Bear's Hair Lure –
UK. Cliff Henry design. Strip
of bear hair, on the skin, tied
in by the ribbing.
4 Black Matuka – *NZ/
universal*. Matuka is the style,
with the wing/tail material
secured by turns of ribbing.
Also Red & Black, Yellow,
Green, and Olive. Similar:

Walker's Black Widow
[*Africa*] – red silk body and
jungle cock sides: Black Prince
[*NZ*] – with red tail, red
chenille body, and black
Matuka wing/tail over.
5 Viva – *UK*. Hairwing
version shown. Also tied with
wing of four black cock
hackles, and with silver rib.
Has added tag.
6 Ace of Spades – *UK*. Dave
Collyer pattern, tied Matuka-
style, but with bronze mallard
wing slips over. His Brown
Bomber is similar.
7 Black Zonker – *USA*. Use
of Mylar tinsel to give scale
effect. Wing is black rabbit
fur, on the skin, tied in at
head and tail. Also other
colours. Also a bass fly.

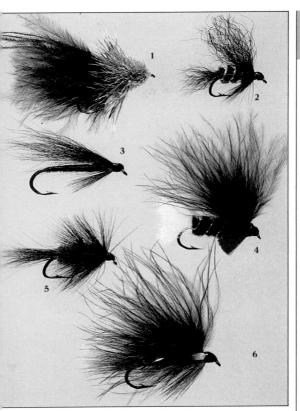

1 Black Marabou Muddler – *USA/UK.* Muddler-style head with marabou dressing. Composite dressings like this include most of the modern popular reservoir lines.

2 Red Hairy Dog – *New Zealand.* Also Green Hairy Dog, and Black Hairy Dog with appropriate colours of body chenille. Initially hair was taken from a spaniel, but now the usual tying is squirrel hair.

3 Sweeney Todd – *UK.* Richard Walker pattern: throat hackle and body segment fluorescent magenta (not fluorescent red) Also Sweeney Doll – **Baby Doll** style with body black 2/3, fluorescent magenta 1/3 black wool over the back.

4 Christmas Tree – *UK.* Reservoir lure, a favourite on Rutland Water; attracting fluorescent green and red added to Black Marabou.

5 Red Fuzzy Wuzzy – *New Zealand.* Also Green Fuzzy Wuzzy – green-bodied. In the larger sizes, the fly is tri-partite.

6 Black & Orange Marabou – *UK.* A strong dash of colour contrast at throat and tail. In early season cold water flies like this are recommended to be fished deep and slow, as the fish, rainbows particularly, will be searching for food near the bottom.

1 *Nandi Bear* – *Kenya.*
Weighted, inverted so as not
to foul up on river or lake bed.
An Unwin's invention.
2 *Makora* – *Kenya.* Variation
on **Viva**. Weighted and upside
down. Another Unwin pattern.
3 *Dudu* – *Kenya.* Adaptation
of **Worm Fly**. Designed by
Unwin's. Similarities to
Dambuster. Weighted and
upside down.
4 *Black Woolly Bugger* –
USA. Mobile marabou tail and
palmered body – suggests
succulent larva, e.g. of black
stonefly, tadpole, or leech.
5 *Montana* (Green
Fluorescent) – *USA/Africa.*
Variation on Montana Nymph.
Weighted or unweighted.
Standard pattern: underside of

thorax is yellow chenille.
Other colour variations. See
also **Ted's Stone**.
6 *Sir Roden's Killer* –
Australia/Tasmania.
Incorporates yellow chenille
body.
7 *Bitch Creek* (Orange) –
USA/Kenya. Of Montana
origin. Either braided back
(mossback) or all-chenille
bodied. Rubber appendages.
Variations: other colours, viz
green. Stonefly nymph
imitation.

1 Girdle Bug – *USA*.
Imagine from the name the
source of the rubber
appendages! Usually medium
to small, dressed with little or
modest extra weight. Similar
to Rubberlegs which is heavier
and larger. Black most
common tying.
2 Friel's Fancy – *Africa*.
3 Hilliard Special – *Africa*.
Compare with **Alexandra**.
4 Walker's Special – *Africa*.
5 Alder – *USA*. Imitation of
Sialis infumata – slightly
darker than the UK alder,
Sialis lutaria. **Leadwing
Coachman** a possible pattern.
The larval form surprisingly, is
not dark-brown/blackish. See
Alder Larva.
6 Black Nymph – *USA*.

Folded quill thorax, black
wool body. compare with UK
pattern: red in thorax and
black seal's fur body.
7 Black Snail – *UK*. A Cliff
Henry pattern, with cork or
closed-cell foam body. Body
should be drenched in varnish.
8 Black Creeper – *Japan*.
Dorsal view.
9 Black & Peacock Spider –
UK. Tom Ivens pattern.
Immensely successful. Good
when snails are about.
Possibly a representation of
beetles.
10 Eric's Beetle – *UK*. Eric
Horsefall Turner's pattern for
the River Derwent – widely
accepted for river and
stillwater use. Either just
below the suface or well sunk.

1 Black Swannundaze Stone – *General*. In many colours. Incorporates plastic material, flat on one side and half oval on the other.
2 Giant Black Stonefly Nymph – *USA*. Natural is *Pteronarcys dorsata*, 2in maximum growth, with a 3-year underwater life cycle. Emerges in early June.
3 Early Black Stonefly Larva – *USA*. Natural is *Capnia vernalis*. Emerges late winter.
4 Kuromagara-Kagero – *Japan*. Variation on mossback style. ¾ view.
5 Dark Mossback – *USA*. Does a good job imitating the Montana "salmon fly". A Dan Bailey pattern. ¾ view.

6 Black Leech – *UK*. As with tadpole imitations, worth a pattern in the flybox. ¾ view.
7 Colonel's Black Creeper – *Kenya*. Generalized deep weighted pattern of insect-type to attract large game fish. Designed to swim hook point upwards. Other colours.
8 Kenya Bug – *Africa*. Much African tying development is to present large succulent morsels – beetle larvae, dragonfly larvae, etc.
9 Craig's Nighttime – *New Zealand*. Removal of the brighter elements results in a beetle/grub-like form.
10 Black Phantom – *New Zealand*. Jungle cock sides an option. Body colour: black chenille, silver rib.

1 Duck Fly Nymph –
Ireland. Chironomid
interpretation. Body material
also seal's fur or wool. Ribs
silver or gold. Some patterns
have "legs".
2 Black Buzzer – *UK*.
Standard pattern, also in Red,·
Green, etc.
3 Red-tipped Black Buzzer
– *UK*. Another variation on
the Black Buzzer is Richard
Walker's Red-ringed Black
Buzzer. The red ring is behind
the thorax.
**4 Black Hatching Buzzer
Pupa** – *UK*. Style also in
Green, Red, etc. Trout are
occasionally exceptionally
selective, so alternative
patterns are worth carrying.
5 Black Hatching Midge –

UK. Moment of emergence.
Also Red, Brown, Green etc.
6 Maury's Nymph – *Africa*.
Maury is Maurice Wilson with
many African patterns to his
credit.
7 Ti-tree Beetle –
Australia/Tasmania. There are
fewer upwings in the Southern
Hemisphere, so many good
trout patterns represent
terrestrials.
8 Black Beetle –
Australia/Tasmania. Wing
cases envelop the top of the
hackle.
9 St Hans Flua –
Norway/Denmark/Sweden.
10 Black Ant –
Australia/Tasmania. See also
dry patterns. Rather old-
fashioned in tying style.

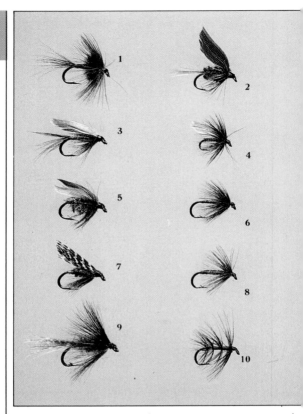

1 *Black Gnat Nymph* – *New Zealand*. Somewhat bulkier than the similar UK Black Gnat Nymph.

2 *Pomahaka Black* – *New Zealand*. Tying named after the Pomahaka River in South Island. Tied wet and dry.

3 *Cairn's Fancy* – *Scotland*. A fly of many names: in Ireland, Blue Body Black Hackle; in the north of England, Broughton's Point. Dressed larger, it is Bluebottle.

4 *Black Gnat* – *UK*. Small, blackish, sometimes winged. Wing colours and materials vary.

5 *Bluebottle* – *UK*. Serves to represent other small dark insects as well, aquatic or terrestrial.

6 *Murray's Bluebottle* – *Scotland*. Bluebottles (*Diptera*) are not aquatic insects but an imitation can be handy.

7 *Harrison's Bluebottle* – *Africa*. The heavily veined wings of the natural are imitated here with a teal wing.

8 *Black Spider* – *UK*. Sparsely dressed as a wet fly. Also tied as a dry fly. With black tail whisks constitutes Williams' Favourite.

9 *Ricky's Mole* – *Africa*. Heavily picked-out body.

10 *Stewart's Black Spider* – *Scotland*. Extreme mobility in the hackling. Designed for upstream wet-fly fishing.

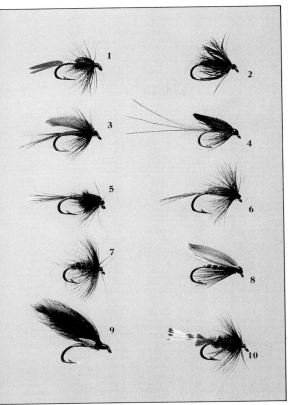

1 Butcher Nymph – *UK*. See
Butcher. This dressing
adapted to nymph style.
2 Staple Diet – *Africa*.
Coarse-fibre hackle, rather
than cock or hen hackle. Stout
wool body.
3 Ronald – *Scotland*. Black
Gnat style, but with red
afterbody.
4 Red Body Waipahi – *New
Zealand*. Note long tail whisks
and mallard speculum wing.
Named after South Island
river.
5 Black's Nymph – *New
Zealand*.
6 Nymbeet – *Australia/
Tasmania*. Also tied with
greyish black body. Pattern
started as a water beetle larva
imitation. Also seems to

represent shrimp-type
naturals.
7 Dark Sedge – *New Zealand*.
8 Isflua – *Norway/Denmark/
Sweden*. Also tied as a floater.
9 Robin – *Australia/
Tasmania*.
10 Ke-He (Black) – *Scotland*.
A pattern designed by Kemp
and Heddle for the Orkney
Loch Harray. Variations
include addition of red tuft to
tail. Also Ke-He (Brown) with
natural red hackle instead of
black. Also Severn Ke, a
Welsh adaptation with a white
cock hackle.

1 *Blae & Black* (silver rib) –
UK. A standard Irish wet
pattern for lake and sea-trout
fishing. The Blae & Silver
differs in having a pale badger
hackle and flat silver tinsel
body.
2 *Teal & Black* – *UK/general*.
A good black chironomid
imitation.
3 *Prince Charming* – *Africa*.
Similarities to ***Butcher***.
4 *Connemara Black* –
Ireland. Sometimes tied with
silver wire and yellow floss
tag. One of Ireland's favourite
sea-trout and lake trout flies.
5 *Black Pennell* – *UK*.
Important traditional loch fly.
Also for sea-trout, in which
section see styles for dapping
and bob fly.

6 *Yate's Silver* – *Africa*.
Similarities to ***Butcher***.
7 *Nessie* – *New Zealand*.
8 *Sepia Nymph* – *UK*.
Similar to claret nymph. This
upwing is an early emerger
from still waters – from early
April.
9 *Tadpolly* – *UK*. Tadpole
imitation from John Goddard.
10 *Tadpole* – *UK*. Imitation
of the young of frogs and
toads. Tied with silk or
marabou body extensions;
built-up or slender heads.
Variety of sizes in different
patterns.

1 Love's Lure – *New Zealand.*
A South Island pattern with
beetle overtones.
2 Jessie No 1 – *New Zealand.*
The postmaster at Kakahi
allegedly named the flies in
this series after Jessie
Freeman. Fancy rather than
specifically imitative.
3 Adams – *USA.* Shows a
pattern that quite closely
approximates patterns of
other countries. Also similar,
Hardy's Favourite. See dry.
4 Jessie No 4 – *New Zealand.*
Black silk body, not peacock.
5 Ivor's Special – *Africa.*
Very similar to **Hardy's
Favourite.**
6 Gorbenmac – *Africa.*
7 Evans Peacock – *Africa.*
Note name is EVANS

PEACOCK, not Evans
Chameleon. Pattern from Vic
Evans, doyen of Natal fly
fishers. Unfortunately
misnamed in Veniard's
invaluable *A further guide to
fly dressing.*
8 King Butcher – *Africa.*
Variation from standard
Butcher by use of white-
tipped mallard wing and
inclusion of tippet fibres to
tail. Classically tied with
secondary feathers from the
wing of the lilac-breasted
roller.
9 Black Palmer –
UK/universal. Early
traditional tying. With red tag
is **Black Zulu.** Also tied dry.
10 Gray Hackle – *USA.*
Standard non-specific nymph.

1 Walker's Killer – *Africa*.
Inventor Lionel Walker
wanted a solid morsel for big
trout. Body, red chenille.
Wing, 18 tips of partridge
hackles (3 layers of 3 feathers
each) at equal intervals along
the shank. Fly must maintain
a shape of streamlined bulk.
2 Pombe King – *Kenya*.
Adaptation of Walker's Killer,
with added weight, and tied to
be fished upside down. Also
Pombe Queen – wings set like
Mrs Simpson, weighted,
upside down.
3 Mrs Simpson (Red) – *New
Zealand*. Variation on the
"killer" style in that the flank
feathers do not fully overlap
those tied in before. Also Mrs
Simpson Yellow, and Mrs

Simpson Fluorescent Green.
Arguably named after Edward
VIII and Mrs Simpson, who
visited New Zealand.
4 Socdologer – *Africa*. Rich
brownish red seal's fur body.
5 Lord's Killer – *New
Zealand*. Body red chenille in
illustration; also yellow, green,
or orange. Woodcock feather
flanks.
6 Koppe Braun – *Germany*.
"Killer"-style interpretation
from Germany. Body: black
chenille, ribbed gold. Also
Koppe Grau, with grey
mallard flanks.
7 Kilwell No 2 – *New
Zealand*. Yellow wool body on
example illustrated. Also red.
8 Leslie's Lure – *New
Zealand*. Deep red wool body.

1 Matuka Muddler – *New Zealand*. Imitation of small riverbed-living bait fish. American influence on the style notable in the construction of the head. New Zealand influence in the tail and winging. Expect variations by local fly tiers.

2 Lead-headed Mayfly Lure – *UK*. The "explosion" of marabou into attractor dressings has only been recent, although the style of pulsing mobile feather has been known a long time. The addition of extra weight, in the manner of American lead-headed jigs, makes the fly rise and fall in a sinuous fashion with the marabou fibres intensifying the style of progression. The patterns are basic and extremely popular for fishing for rainbows in rivers and stillwaters. Trials have not been long-term enough for proof of these flies in fishing for salmon or sea-trout. Another name for them, patented, is Dog Nobbler, prefixed by the appropriate colour or other designation.

3 Dave's Sculpin – *USA*. Small river-bed living bait fish imitation. Dave is David Whitlock, who first tested the pattern on the White River in Arkansas. May be weighted. An example of the Muddler style with considerable development. Illustrated ¾ view.

1 Mylar Minnow – *UK*. Syd Brock reservoir pattern, similar in style to **Polystickle** and **Jersey Herd**.
2 Zug Bug – *USA*. Broad-spectrum imitation of larger subaquatics. "Tails" on a number of insects in their subaquatic immature stage are often gill elements, heavily fibrous. Examples are dragonfly nymphs.
3 Kerr's Special – *Africa*.
4 Perille – *Germany*. Almost an excess use of peacock herls.
5 Finnish Spider – *Finland*. "Spider": compared with American and British terminologies. The eight-legged insect is meant here.
6 Natural Mayfly Nymph – *UK*. Very markedly different

from Richard **Walker's Mayfly Nymph**.
7 Cream Latex Sedge Pupa – *UK*. Differs from American style; no stub downward-orientated wings. Either "natural" colour latex is wound over a base colour of a different tone, or latex may be coloured or marked with indelible pens. Longer lasting than rubber-band type rubber.
8 Cream Latex Nymph – *USA/Japan*. Hackle and wings at junction of body with thorax.
9 Special Nymph No 2 – *Japan*.
10 Special Nymph No 3 – *Japan*. Buoyancy from closed-cell foam bow-tie.

1 Mayfly Nymph – *New Zealand*. Very similar to the patterns of mayfly nymphs sold in the 1950s, but now superseded by more modern imitations.

2 Caddis Fly Nymph – *New Zealand*. Extended body, possible in most wet and dry fly styles.

3 Stonefly Nymph – *New Zealand*. See **Dark Stone** p. 40.

4 Brown Sedge – *New Zealand*.

5 Black Sedge Pupa – *UK*. Brownish wing and thorax, rather than black throughout as might have been expected.

6 Early Brown Stonefly Nymph – *USA*. Similar are **Colonel's Creeper** (Hare's Ear) and **Swannundaze** (Hare's Ear). Simulates *Taeniopteryx nivalis* or *T. occidentalis*.

7 Coch-y-bondhu – *Wales/general*. Initially an imitation of the beetle living in the heather of the Welsh hillsides. The latest and probably accurate spelling is Coch-a-bon-ddu.

8 Coch-y-bondhu Beetle – *Wales/general*. Wing case included.

9 Higenaga – *Japan*. Weighted.

10 Picket Pin – *USA*. Tied originally with gopher tail hair – called Picket Pin because this little ground squirrel sitting upright resembles a picket pin.

39

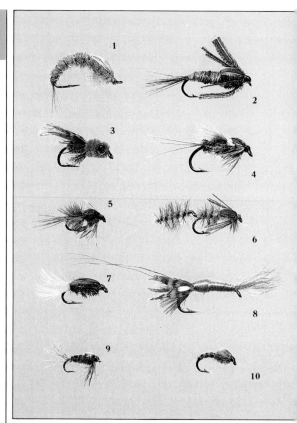

**1 Gold-Ribbed Hare's Ear
Larva** – *France.* Although the
GRHE is normally recognized
as an imitation in nymph,
emerger or dun form of
various olives, this much
larger, curved artificial relates
far more closely to caddis
pupae and larvae.
2 Dark Stone – *New Zealand.*
Some of the South Island
streams are particularly rich in
Plecoptera. Main kinds are the
long-tailed *Zelandoperla
maculata*, short-tailed
Auklandobius trivacuata, and
the green *Stenoperla prasina.*
3 Mudeye (*Feathered*) –
Australia/Tasmania. Dragonfly
larvae form a large part of
Australian/Tasmanian trout
diet.
4 Emerging Nymph –
Africa.
5 Arthofer Nymphe –
Germany.
6 Wiggle Nymph – *USA.*
Originating with Swisher and
Richards (or with Bill Blades).
Also responsible for no-hackle
dry fly experimentation.
7 Nut-brown Beetle No 1 –
Africa.
8 Popeye-the-prawn –
Africa. Compare with salmon
prawn flies, and also with the
Latex Prawn (Japan) for
style.
9 Special Nymph (8) –
Japan.
10 Beige Flexibody Buzzer
– *UK.* "Flexibody" is a
modern fly-tying non-natural
material. In many colours.

1 Jennings Nymph – *USA.*
Large non-specific. May
regularly be weighted.
2 Yate's Standby – *Africa.*
3 Half Back – *New Zealand.*
Weighted pattern. Tony
Orman in *Trout with Nymph*
lists this as a general pattern
with considerable popularity
in the Taupo district (North
Island), as well as elsewhere.
4 Perla – *New Zealand.* A
stonefly nymph or larva
imitation, as its name
suggests.
**5 Stewart's Dark Spanish
Needle** – *UK.* The highly
mobile style of Stewart's for
this small stonefly imitation.
6 Back Swimmer –
Australia/Tasmania. Natural
also called water boatman.

7 Little Sand Sedge – *USA.*
Goera americana pupates in
late March in western streams.
There was a Scottish artificial,
Corncrake & Yellow, but more
modern tyings separate body
and thorax, and include stub
wings.
8 Barrie Welham Nymph –
UK. Designed by Barrie
Welham, notable caster and
fisherman. Tied by Peter
Deane in slender (shown) and
stout profiles.
9 Nymphe Typ D – *Germany.*
Strong element of **Sawyer
Pheasant Tail Nymph** in the
wire thorax.
10 Stick Caddis –
Australia/Tasmania. Compare
with **Stick Fly** and the many
cased caddis styles illustrated.

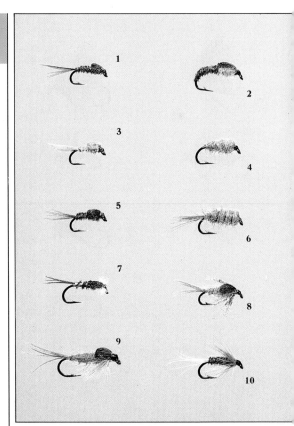

1 Sawyer's Pheasant Tail Nymph – *UK*. Frank Sawyer, river keeper on the Avon, devised four nymph/bug patterns of extreme tying simplicity, of reasonable verisimilitude, and with enough weight to sink quickly and unobtrusively.

2 Cove's Pheasant Tail Nymph – *UK*. A long shank hook, and dressing curled on round towards the barb.

3 Sawyer's Grey Goose Nymph – *UK*. Later in the season the **PT Nymph** is too dark, and goose quill over copper wire represents the paler olives admirably.

4 Sawyer's Killer Bug – *UK*. The hook shank is wrapped with copper wire and Chadwick's 477 wool.

5 Sawyer's Scandinavian Nymph – *UK*. A larger and darker version of the **Grey Goose Nymph**.

6 Copper & Hare Nymph – *New Zealand*. Very similar to **Killer Bug**; copper ribbing.

7 Sawyer's Bowtie Buzzer – *UK*. This imitation hangs vertically and will twitch attractively.

8 Quill Gordon – *USA*. Also Gordon Quill as alternative standard names. Natural known as blue quill, grey quill.

9 All-purpose Medium Nymph – *UK*. Orvis pattern – general wide-spectrum upwing nymph series.

10 Pheasant Tail – *UK*. Most useful all-purpose fly.

1 Leadwing Coachman Nymph – *USA*. The style relates more closely to beetle or dragonfly larvae than to upwing forms.

2 Prince – *USA*. Broad spectrum larva/nymph imitation. Usually weighted.

3 Ombudsman – *UK*. Brian Clarke pattern, to suggest a number of creatures like alder larvae or caddis.

4 Alder Larva – *UK*. Immature *Sialis lutaria*. Some tyings are paler with more emphasis on the pale gill elements. Sometimes weighted.

5 Stick Fly – *General*. General caddis, alder larva, dragonfly nymph type artificial.

6 Twitchett Nymph – *General*. With added weight, cased caddis type artificial, with tag of fluorescent green.

7 Mahogany – *USA*. From the Orvis Index. Natural: *Isonychia bicolor*, also commonly known as the leadwing coachman.

8 Welsh Partridge – *UK*. A Courtney Williams design which he thoroughly recommended as a good general pattern on all but chalksteams.

9 Snipe & Purple – *UK*. North country pattern, particularly successful as an iron blue imitation.

10 Greenwell's Spider – *UK*. General purpose olive imitation, either as dun or nymph. A very important artificial worldwide.

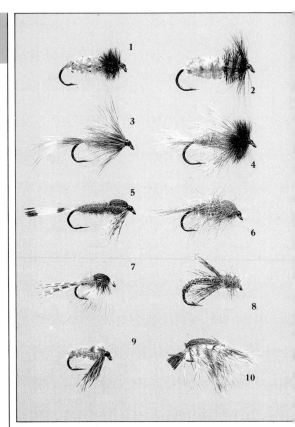

1 Caddis Case Larva – *USA.*
The caddis grub inhabits a
case of gravel or vegetation.
Its head and legs protrude.
The imitation should be fished
close to the bottom.
2 Caddis Case Larva –
Germany. Despite the same
name as the preceding pattern,
the case is distinctly pink.
3 Gray Nymph – *USA.* This
is the Lee Wulff nymph of the
Gray Wulff floater. A
generalized upwing nymph
pattern.
4 Casual Dress – *USA.*
Caddis-type pattern. May be
weighted.
5 Himefutao-Kagero –
Japan. Very similar to the
Orvis All-purpose Dark
Nymph.

**6 Gold-ribbed Hare's Ear
Nymph** – *USA/UK.* In USA
body made from rabbit fur. In
UK, a non-specific general
purpose nymph.
7 Zero – *Japan.* Not to be
confused with UK reservoir
lure Zero devised by Steve
Parton to resemble bream fry,
similar to the **Appetiser**.
8 Rising Caddis Nymph –
Germany. Very much more
slender than imitations from
other countries.
9 Blue Dun Nymph (Dark) –
New Zealand. Probable choice
of pattern to imitate upwings
Deleatidium spp and *Zephlebia*
spp, although the Sawyer
patterns might be preferred.
10 Shrimp – *Africa.* See also
Chomper and **Shrimper**.

1 Roman Moser Sedge Pupa – *Germany*. Traun Tackle Company winging material. Versatile enough for upwing and sedge winging duties.

2 Sand's Favourite – *Norway/Denmark/Sweden*. Very similar to **March Brown Spider**.

3 Silversedge Pupa – *France*. Central hackle rather than stub wings.

4 Dusty Nymph Grizzly – *USA/Japan*.

5 Nymphe Typ B – *Germany*. Similar in style to **Sawyer's Grey Goose Nymph**, but with gold wire showing under the thorax.

6 Stick Caddis – *New Zealand*. Compares with **Stick Caddis** (*Australia/Tasmania*) and **Stick Insect**.

7 Musson's Mephistopheles – *Africa*. Use of gallina (guinea fowl) hackle.

8 Zebra Nymph – *Switzerland*. Copper wire in body.

9 Poil de Lièvre – *France*. Hare's pelt. Rather noticeably different from USA and UK patterns of **Gold-ribbed Hare's Ear**.

10 Hedgehog – *UK*. Richard Walker development. It can either be tied in shape or size to correspond with the trout pellet, or to imitate the snail. Muddler-head spun deer hair.

1 February Red – *Ireland*.
Natural is *Taeniopteryx
nebulosa*, known as the red fly
and Old Joan – a member of
the Perlidae. Considered to be
the Dun Fly of the *Treatise*
(1496). The Partridge &
Orange is an alternative.
2 Lensmannsflua –
Norway/Denmark/Sweden.
3 Mustad's Favourite –
Norway/Denmark/Sweden.
Quite similar to **Mallard &
Silver**. Silver tail elements.
4 Heggeli –
Norway/Denmark/Sweden.
Similarities to **Mallard &
Silver**.
5 Palsbu – *Norway*.
6 Murray's Favourite – *New
Zealand*. Similar to **Jessie**
patterns.

7 March Brown Variant –
Africa. The March Brown in
its many forms is one of the
best general purpose flies
around. It manages,
depending on the way it is
fished, to imitate upwing
nymphs, caddis pupae or
shrimp types, or drowned
duns.
8 Mini Muddler Minnow –
USA/general. Full size, the
pattern appears like a small
fish. In miniature it can
represent a sedge, a sedge
pupa or a moth.
9 Olsen – *Norway*. Very
similar to **Woodcock &
Mixed**.
10 Harlequin – *Scotland*.
Blae-type wing with mixed-
type body.

1 Sugar Daddy – *New Zealand*. Similar to Thundercreek style. See **Black-nosed Dace**.

2 Golden Darter – *USA*. Companion to **Silver Darter**, but darker, as expected.

3 Bishop's Blessing – *New Zealand*. Preference is for it to be tied with pale feathers.

4 Lady Ghost – *USA/Canada*. This has reproduced in the photograph slightly paler than its tying. One of the char/steelhead/landlocked salmon patterns that may be tied up to $4\frac{1}{2}$ inches long, and in tandems.

5 Lévrière – *France*.

6 Brown Woolly Worm – *USA*. Tops the list of many US nymph fishers as a good large larval imitation, generally categorized as a nymph, completely unspecifically. It comes in olive, green, orange, black, etc., with a palmered grizzle hackle to give the impression of movement. Charles E. Brooks, in *The Trout and the Stream*, selects these patterns for rapids pockets. Sometimes weighted.

7 Humla – *Norway/Denmark/Sweden*. Compare for style with **Black Pennell, Claret Pennell**, etc.

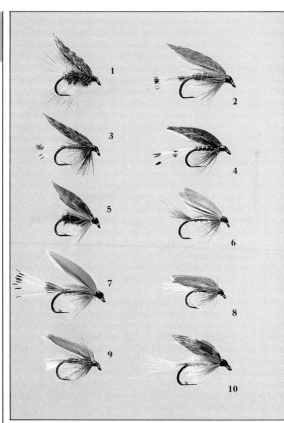

1 Kelso – *USA*. Body with long palmer hackle.
2 Grouse & Purple – *UK/General*. One of the Grouse & . . . series. Used less widely than the Mallard series, and **Grouse & Claret** or **Mallard & Claret** are probably more popular.
3 Purple Grouse – *New Zealand*. See also Grouse series. Optional black or natural red throat hackle on UK tyings.
4 Devil – *Ireland*. Alternative wing, cinnamon hen. The slip of purple included in the wing is a Co. Sligo addition. Black Devil: black floss, and scarlet wing addition. Green Devil: green floss, and emerald wing addition.

5 Red-tip Governor – *New Zealand*. See also USA's: Improved Governor: dark turkey wing, red tip to body, and red tail.
6 Gullflua – *Norway*. Resembles **Wickham's Fancy**, which is palmer hackled.
7 Cinnamon & Gold – *UK*. Favoured lake fly and proven sea-trout fly.
8 Hamilton's Favourite – *New Zealand*. Commemorates Captain G.D. Hamilton, NZ fisher in early 20thC.
9 Colonel Downman – *Scotland*. Top of Hardy's 1937 for trout in Loch Leven.
10 March Brown – *USA*. Not the same fly as in the UK. US is either *Stenomena vicarium* or *Ephemera compar*.

1 Leadwing Coachman –
USA/UK/general. The dullness
of the wing can produce fish
when the standard white-
winged pattern scares them.
Generalized pattern.
2 Coachman – *UK*. The wet
tying is more familiar to many
anglers than the dry, and the
feather-winged pattern the
standard. A hackled pattern is
tied with the white wing
omitted, and a white throat
hackle placed in front of the
natural red.
3 Outspan Coachman –
Africa. Massive white tail and
bold red rib mark the
variation from the original
standard pattern.
4 Kate McLaren – *Scotland*.
Tied for bob-fly use.

5 Dark Sedge Fly – *Ireland*.
A generalized pattern
embracing red sedges,
cinnamon sedges, etc.
6 Swazi Queen – *Africa*.
Some resemblance to
Californian Coachman.
7 Little Redwing – *Africa*.
For wing: substitute woodcock
if South African redwing
partridge not available.
8 Straw Grouse – *Ireland*.
Similar style to Grouse & . . .
series, with addition of red
underwing.
9 Heiber's Sgebenga –
Africa. Very similar to original
Muddler Minnow, but without
the clipped deer hair head.
10 Jindabyne – *Africa*.
Similar to John Ketley's
Allrounder (*UK*).

49

1 Light Cahill – *USA*. Also Light Cahill Nymph. Pattern designed by Dan Cahill and developed by Theodore Gordon. Imitates *Stenonema canadense* and *S. ithaca*.
2 Dark Cahill – *USA*. Nearer the original Cahill dressing, which has progressively been tied lighter.
3 Klara Fly – *Norway*.
4 Auld Hen – *Scotland*. A Tweed pattern similar to Webster's Musk Brown. Recommended as a night fly by Lawrie.
5 August Dun – *UK*. Fly from rivers and stillwaters – *Ecdyonurus dispar*. Body brownish, represented by herls, dubbings or silk. Body dark red in the spinners. Also

known as the autumn dun.
6 Dark Hendrickson – *USA*. Natural: *Leptophlebia cupida*, also called black quill. **Whirling Dun** (*USA*) recommended by Schwiebert to imitate the female dun.
7 Light Hendrickson – *USA*. Nearer the original dressing, which represents *Ephemerella invaria*, the female.
8 Sand Fly – *Germany*. Recommended by Ronalds as a good grayling and dace fly.
9 Verre en Minken – *Norway*.
10 Quill Gordon – *USA*. Female sometimes tied with yellow egg-sac; slightly larger and paler than the male.

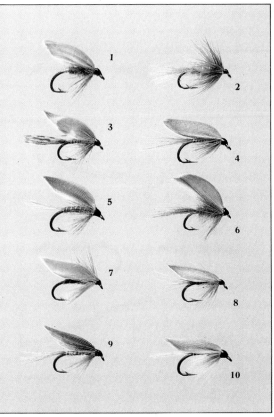

1 Cowdung – *UK/USA*.
Terrestrial: imitation of
orange/olive fly attendant on
cowpats. Occasionally alights
on river or still water.
2 Muskrat – *USA*. Muskrat
fur in America has the same
popularity as mole or water
vole fur in the UK. The result
is a number of general
patterns pressed into use for
specific occasions.
3 Anderson – *New Zealand*.
4 Red Quill – *USA*. See under
Red Quill (dry) for caption to
UK fly of this name. Pattern
also tied with hackle-stalk
body; with woodduck wing;
with dun hackle.
5 Red Spinner – *UK*. The
female imago of *Baëtis
rhodani*, the large dark olive,

correctly is the sole insect of
this name.
6 Whirling Dun – *Australia/
Tasmania*.
7 Krogsgaard – *Denmark*.
8 Dad's Favourite – *New
Zealand*. The original pattern
was fancied only by an
Invercargill butcher, who sent
his son to do his fly buying.
9 Akreflua – *Norway*.
10 Ginger Quill – *USA*.
Natural – *Stenonema fuscum*,
known as ginger quill or gray
fox.

1 Silver & Blue Parrot – *UK*. Also Black, White, Red, Orange, and Green. Mylar silver body.

2 Blae & Silver – *Scotland*. One of the Blae & . . . series, blae referring to the wing colour. Variation: badger throat hackle not blue. Also Blae & Gold, Blae & Grey, Blae Orange & Blue. The dressing illustrated is called Blae & Blue in Ireland.

3 Pesciolino Bleu – *Italy*. Also Pesciolino Rosso, with red wing.

4 Scotch Poacher – *New Zealand*. Tied with or without jungle cock sides. Body orange chenille. A design by John Kirkpatrick of Rotorua, called by a friend "an old Scotch poacher", hence the nickname attached to the fly, which is an established night pattern.

5 Silver Minnow – *France*. Compare for style with **Mylar Minnow**, **Polystickle**, and with the wide range of blue/silver sea-trout flies.

6 Taihape Tickler – *New Zealand*. A pattern invented by Frank Lord of Roturua who combined the ingredients of two good night flies – **Craig's Nighttime** and **Mallard & Claret**.

7 Mestowat – *Kenya*. Upside-down and weighted. Many of these large African patterns have been designed by Unwins.

1 Telemarkskongen –
Norway/Denmark/Sweden.
Compare particularly with the
trout and sea-trout **Teal Blue
& Silver** pattern.
2 Silver Doctor – *Norway/
Denmark/Sweden*. Also tied
dry. There are many trout,
sea-trout and steelhead
patterns of this name, all
derivatives of the **Silver
Doctor** salmon fly.
3 Spencer Bay – *USA/
Canada*. Cream badger wings
suggests similarity with **Lady
Ghost**, **Yorks Kennebago**
and **Spruce**. Tied miniature
for illustration.
4 Sølvdokka – *Norway/
Denmark/Sweden*. More
involved trout dressing,
almost a miniature salmon fly.

5 Fiesta – *Japan*. Streamer
pattern with unravelled Mylar
body material forming tail.
6 Ilen Blue – *Japan*. Similar
to **Bloody Butcher** (*UK*), but
with wing colour approxi-
mating that of some versions
of the Kingfisher Butcher.
7 Nancy – *USA/Canada*.
Landlock streamer, also good
for lake trout; up to 4½ inches;
tandems. Tied in miniature.
8 Nine-Three – *USA/Canada*.
This is definitely my favourite
landlocked salmon lure,
followed closely by the **Gray
Ghost**. Original tying
instructions insist on the green
wing hackles lying flat, and
the black wing hackles lying
on edge above them. Tied up
to very large sizes.

1 Leprechaun – *UK*. Tied either streamer style, as shown, or matuka style. Body is lime-green fluorescent, which has an illogical attraction for trout.
2 Hamill's Killer (Red) – *New Zealand*. Body colour red chenille. Also yellow version. Possible imitation of the bullhead baitfish, or even dragonfly nymph.
3 Green Orbit – *New Zealand*. Similar to Green Matuka and Green Ghost. Also Red Orbit and Yellow Orbit; designs from Wilfred Beaumont-Orr.
4 Green Marabou – *UK*. A wide range of dyed colours is available usually with chenille bodies coloured like the wing.

The name is generalized. These tyings are now standards for reservoir brown and rainbow trout.
5 Woolly Monster – *UK*. Use of fur or hair "on the strip" to make wings. Style found in many colours and textures.
6 Tom Jones – *Australia/ Tasmania*. Of the **Rabbit** style, nearly. Tufts of dyed rabbit fur tied in at head and tail, rather than matuka style.
7 Damselfly Nymph – *USA*. Weighted. Marabou tail gives the effect of the nymph pulsing through the water.
8 Latex Stonefly Nymph – *USA*. There are a number of green/olive stonefly nymphs, e.g., *Chloroperla coloradensis* and *C. pallidula*.

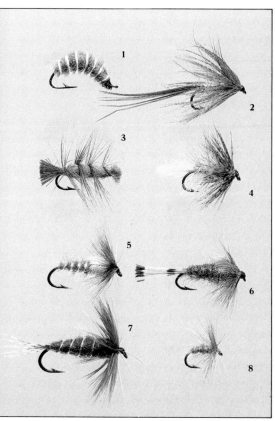

1 Caterpillar – *UK*. The small green caterpillars that hang from threads are the most likely to fall into the water. This is just one of many patterns in green, red, olive and brown.
2 Olive Hackled Wet Mayfly – *Ireland*. This style is straddlebug – extra long projecting hackle to be finished ungreased in the surface film.
3 Raupe (Caterpillar) – *Germany*. Very similar to **Woolly Worm**.
4 Olive Palmer – *UK*. Very similar to the Irish Partridge & Yellow, a good lake pattern.
5 Olive Sedge Pupa – *UK*. In similar style: Green, Orange, Cream, and Brown.

This style is easily tied and is a UK standard dressing.
6 Green Stone Fly – *New Zealand*. Weighted pattern. The natural is *Stenoperla prasina*. Jim Ring's Green Stonefly Nymph is very similar. $\frac{3}{4}$ view.
7 Small's Green Nymph – *Africa*. Probable water beetle or dragonfly nymph imitation.
8 Green Sedge – *New Zealand*. This is a free-living caddis, crawling around unprotected by any case. It is up to 20mm long and found in fairly rapid streams.

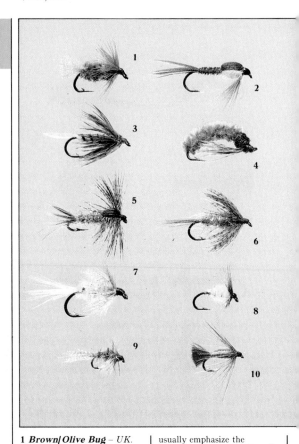

1 Brown/Olive Bug – *UK*.
Weighted.
**2 Green Fluorescent
Pheasant Tail Nymph** –
UK. In same style,
Fluorescent Orange Pheasant
Tail Nymph. Both derived
from *Sawyer's Pheasant
Tail Nymph* but much
enlarged for reservoir use, with
extra attractor colour.
3 Green Beast – *UK*.
Imitates a waterbeetle larva,
an invention of Alan Pearson.
Worthwhile in a much smaller
version as well.
4 Olive Hunchback – *New
Zealand*. Also Brown
Hunchback in this style.
Caddis (sedge) pupa imitation.
5 Rising Nymph – *Germany*.
6 Demoiselle – *UK*. Patterns

usually emphasize the
breathing elements of the tail
appendages, the slender body
and long legs.
7 Walker's Green Nymph –
Africa. A darker version has
black tail fibres and black
cock throat hackle.
**8 Fluorescent Green
Nymph** – *UK*. Kept simple
with no tail fibres.
9 CK Nymphe – *Germany*.
Use of mallard for tail fibres,
and badger throat hackle.
10 Palaretta Grün –
Germany. Fly adopted by
Germany from France. Also
Gelb – yellow.

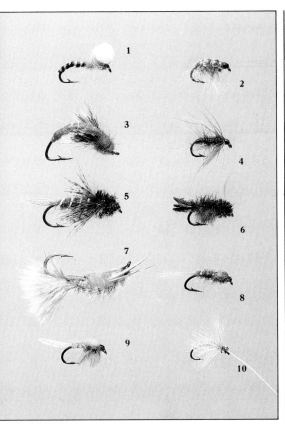

1 Suspender Buzzer Bright Green Flexibody – *UK*. A polystyrene bead gives buoyancy as the artificial hangs at the required angle on the underside of the surface film.
2 Shrimper – *UK*. Designed for the reservoir fisherman, this pattern can be tied in a variety of shades.
3 Green Latex Pupa – *USA*.
4 Dark Seal's Fur Olive – *UK*. Soft hackle pattern of the Stewart style. General ephemerid nymph representation.
5 Dragonfly – *General*. Extra bulk distinguishes purpose-built imitations from generalized demoiselle/dragonfly imitations.

6 Ivens' Brown & Green Nymph – *UK*. If fished fast may be taken by trout as a small fish.
7 Colonel's Creeper (Olive) – *Kenya/general*. A combination of styles: marabou, biots, plus weight and inverted design. Wide colour range.
8 Green Nymph SF – *Africa*. Picked out seal's fur body.
9 Collyer's Green Nymph – *UK*. Under-thorax of dyed ostrich herl. Series: Brown Nymph, Black Nymph, Grey Nymph.
10 Camiole No 12 – *Italy*. One of an immense series of Italy wet trout and grayling flies, some tied with bead head. Often dressed on eyeless hooks.

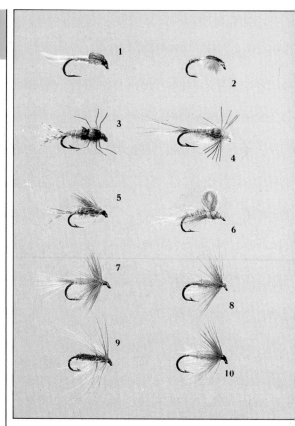

1 PVC Nymph – *UK*.
Goddard-designed pattern
with body of dyed herl
overlaid with pvc strip.
Thorax and underbody of
copper wire to add weight.
2 Olive & Gold Nymph –
UK. One of a nymph series:
also Orange & Gold, Claret &
Gold.
3 Olive Upright Nymph
(Burgess) – *UK*. Raffene or
equivalent thorax and back,
nylon legs. ¾ view.
4 Marabou Nymph – *UK*.
Doug Cooper series. Marabou
fibres twisted together make
the body and are allowed to
project under the thorax.
5 Hatching Nymph –
Ireland. Fished in the surface
film.

6 Olive Floating Nymph –
USA. Surface film nymph. In
emergent stage wings starting
to project through thorax.
7 Rough Olive Nymph –
UK/*general*. Rough – a picked-
out fur or wool body, rather
than silk or stripped quill.
8 Corps Dubbing Olive –
France. Picked-out wool or fur
body. Also Corps Dubbing
Gris-grey.
9 Stewart's Olive Bloa –
Scotland. Within the Stewart
style. Notable for the mobility
of the hackle fibre rather than
specific imitation.
10 Bratstroms Flua –
Norway/*Denmark*/*Sweden*.
Olive nymph or green sedge
pupa imitation.

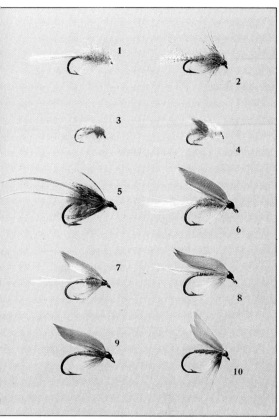

1 *Poil d'Olive* – *France*. Olive
fur or wool teased out in same
style as ***Gold-Ribbed Hare's
Ear***.
**2 *Blue-Winged Olive
Nymph*** – *USA*. Name
borrowed from the UK to
describe easily *Ephemerella
attenuata*.
3 *Green Caddis Larva* –
USA. Schwiebert calls them
"micro caddis", but restricts
himself to 12 patterns to cover
many more naturals. On the
smallest available hooks.
4 *Green Caddis Pupa* –
USA. A style: Cream, Olive,
etc. Sometimes body overlaid
with pvc strip or flat monofil
nylon.
5 *Green Longhorns* – *UK*.
Originally tied with ostrich

herl. Also tied with seal's fur
or lamb's wool.
6 *Olive Dun* – *UK*. A
standard winging style with
dubbed body.
7 *McLeod's Olive* – *Scotland*.
A preference of some tiers – to
add a tinsel tag.
8 *Olive Quill* – *UK*. Equally
as popular as the dry pattern.
9 *Greenwell's Glory* – *UK*.
The body of this most famous
of olive imitations is primrose
tying silk waxed with brown
wax. When wet, the tint
obtained is olive.
10 *Greenwell's* (Split-Wing)
– *UK*. Illustrated from slightly
above. Gives a winged pattern
extra kick. Winging style
recommended by some for
Butcher and other standards.

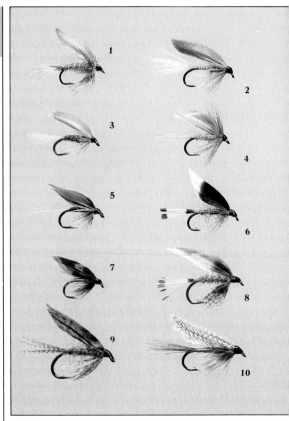

1 Willow Fly – *Scotland*.
Tying very similar to that of
Rough Olive. Not to be
confused with the withy fly or
needle fly which, although
called a willow fly, is actually
a stonefly.
2 Fosskviskflua – *Norway/
Denmark/Sweden*. Combination
of **Rough Olive** and **Olive
Quill**, with a "rough" half of
the body partly hidden by the
throat hackle.
3 Rough Olive – *Scotland*.
Effectively a ribbed Olive
Dun. Imitations of the *Baëtis*
insects range from blue-grey
through greens and olives to
brownish.
4 Burleigh – *Scotland*. "Blae"
wing – alternative pattern to
Grouse & Green and Mallard &

Green.
5 Bungalow Black – *Africa*.
Probably makes excellent
imitation of UK dark olive.
6 Green Heckham Peckham
– *Norway/Denmark/Sweden*.
Variation on the usual red-
bodied Heckham Peckham.
Series designed by William
Murdoch of Scotland.
7 Jessie No 3 – *New Zealand*.
8 Green Partridge –
Scotland. Distinguish from
Partridge & . . . which have
partridge feather throat
hackle, no wing, and are tied
spider style.
9 Game & Green – *Africa*.
10 Grizzly King – *USA*. An
American standard. Also dry.
Variations: steelhead dressings
with hairwing; streamers.

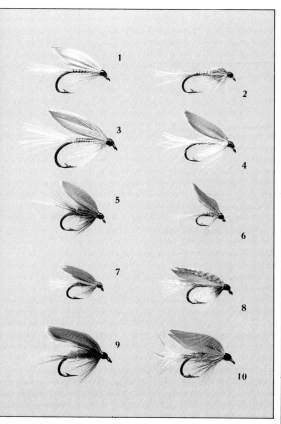

1 Blue Quill – *UK*. Wet or dry, a good chalkstream fly. *USA*: represents *Epeorus pleuralis*, also known as gordon quill, grey quill, and blue dun.

2 Black Quill Nymph – *USA*. To imitate *Leptophlebia cupida*, also known as the dark hendrickson or black quill.

3 Mooi Moth – *Africa*. The Mooi is a notable front river.

4 Fiske-Jo – *Norway*.

5 Iron Blue Dun – *UK*. This small dark ephemerid is one of the most important to the fly fisher. Tied with or without wings, both wet and dry.

6 Blue Hen Quill – *Scotland*. The name differs from the standard **Blue Quill**, but the dressing does not.

7 Blue-Winged Olive – *USA*. Imitation of *Ephemerella attenuata*. UK: imitation of *Ephemerella ignita*.

8 Kakahi Queen – *New Zealand*. North Island pattern. See also dry.

9 Blue Dun – *USA*. Early season upwing known as *Epeorus pleuralis*. Also known as blue quill and grey quill. UK pattern very similar but in a variety of very sparse winging styles, and usually paler.

10 Gold-Ribbed Hare's Ear – *UK*. Non-specific imitation but succeeds in representing olives. Tied dry as well. With or without wings. Possible emerger imitation.

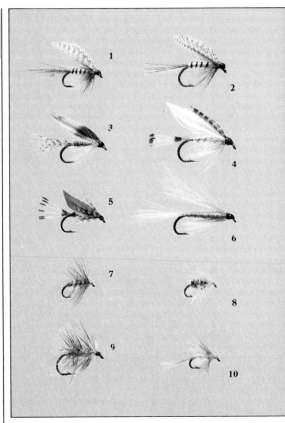

1 Grey Dracke – *Germany.*
2 Mallard & White –
Scotland.
3 Malloch's Favourite –
Scotland.
4 Riinesflua – *Norway/
Denmark/Sweden.*
5 Blue Jay – *Scotland.* Hackle
substitute – for blue jay, use
blue dyed gallina.
6 Tom's Grayling Special –
Norway/Denmark/Sweden.
7 Grayling Steel Blue – *UK.*
General North Country
grayling pattern. Roger
Woolley's original pattern
included three turns of orange
silk at the tail.
8 Yellow Bumble – *UK.*
Grayling standard from the
North Country. Usually tied in
small sizes. Wet and dry.

9 Heather Moth – *Scotland.*
Terrestrial on the water in
Scotland in July and August.
Also tied as a dry pattern. For
sea-trout as well and, dressed
appropriately, for salmon.
10 Border Greenwell's –
UK. Local variation although
the original fly was designed
in that part of the country.
This is paler and browner than
the standard.

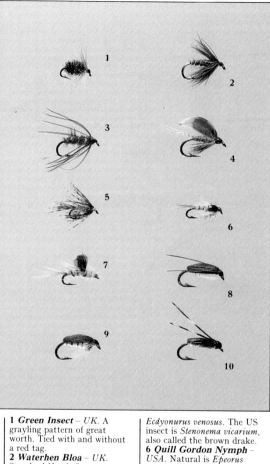

1 Green Insect – *UK*. A
grayling pattern of great
worth. Tied with and without
a red tag.
2 Waterhen Bloa – *UK*.
Standard North Country
pattern for trout and grayling.
Imitation of dark olive or iron
blue. Sparse body.
3 Dark Watchet – *UK*. A
northern standard pattern
representing the iron blue. A
famous trout fly and adequate
grayling fly.
4 Woodcock & Hare's Ear –
UK. Probable resemblance to
sedge pupa or insects such as
march brown.
5 March Brown Spider
(Male) – *Scotland/UK*. The
naturals represented are
Rhithrogena haarupi and

Ecdyonurus venosus. The US
insect is *Stenonema vicarium*,
also called the brown drake.
6 Quill Gordon Nymph –
USA. Natural is *Epeorus
pleuralis*, a frequenter of well
oxygenated streams.
7 Gray Floating Nymph –
USA. Where possible, floating
or just sub-surface flies should
be tied with materials lighter
than water.
8 Corixa (Plastazote) – *UK*.
Closed-cell foam body.
Paddles.
9 Corixa – *UK*. Standard
pattern may include weight.
10 Silver Corixa – *UK*. This
insect swims to the surface to
collect a bubble of air, which
appears silver when held to
the underside of the insect.

1 Green Mallard – *New Zealand*. A design from Geoff Sanderson of Turangi. Body of green wool. Alternative uses grey squirrel tail hair in place of the mallard flank feathers.
2 Roach Fry – *UK*. Contrast with Roach Streamer: white wool body with silver rib, tail dyed red and olive fibres, wing white cock hackles plus olive cock hackles, dyed red throat hackle, Amherst sides, jungle cock cheeks.
3 Blue Devil – *USA/Canada*. In Bergman's recommendations for landlocked salmon and char.
4 Spectraflash Minnow – *Germany*. Getting near the limit of what can be cast with a fly rod, and considered a fly!

5 Gray Ghost – *USA/Canada*. See also under Steelhead section. Is popular now as a reservoir lure in the UK.
6 Grey Ghost (Silver) – *New Zealand*. Smelt/whitebait imitation. Matuka style. Contrast "grey" wing with grey of following patterns. Sometimes eyes are painted onto the head. In the smaller sizes the hackle is sometimes omitted to ensure sleek entry.
7 Grey Ghost (Green) – *New Zealand*. Fluorescent body.
8 Grey Ghost Special – *New Zealand*. Almost blue-green colour, with pronounced yellow wool tag.

1 Cock-a-touche – *Japan.*
More sophisticated **Woolly
Worm**, approximating a small
baitfish like a sculpin.
2 Hare's Fur Swannundaze
– *New Zealand.* A general
pattern utilizing the universal
qualities of hare's fur, and in
the form of a large larva.
Usually weight added.
3 Wizard – *Africa.*
4 Libellen Larva – *Germany.*
Dragonfly larva, pronounced
eyes. Olive and greenish tyings
also. Back made of woven
cloth. There seems a
generalized style for dragonfly
larvae to emphasize the size of
the head. See also **Mudeye**.
5 Mallard Smelt – *New
Zealand.* This is one of Bruno
Kemball's designs. The white-

bodied version is just as
popular.
6 Wesley Special – *USA.*
Landlock pattern. Also for
lake trout; up to 4½ inches.
Tandems. Tied miniature.
7 Jack Spratt – *New Zealand.*
Designed by Jack England,
who had a tackle shop at
Turangi. Jungle cock is
sometimes added. A smelt
imitation.
8 Basil Ross – *New Zealand.*
At much the same time of
year the two major baitfish
are available to the trout:
whitebait (*Galaxias
attenuatus*) and smelt
(*Retropinna*), very similar to
whitebait. A slim small fly
drawn past the feeding trout
usually brings good results.

1 Vulture Matuka – *UK*.
Style from New Zealand.
Smooth, jerk-free retrieve
recommended. Also called
Vulturine Matuka.
2 Three Rivers – *USA/
Canada*. Tied small for the
illustration. Streamer for
landlocked salmon, char, etc.
3 Silver Darter – *USA*. The
use of Mylar tinsel makes this
a particularly effective
minnow imitation. The
pattern is overall lighter in
colour than the **Golden
Darter**, and incorporates a
throat hackle of green peacock
herl.
4 Black Nose Dace – *USA*.
General streamer fly. Tied also
as a steelhead fly. An
imitation of a small bait fish,

Rhinichthys atronsus, common
in the Catskill area.
5 Dainty Veil – *New Zealand*.
Suggestions have been made
that this first half/second half
construction imitates fish eggs
like some steelhead patterns.
6 Ballhead – *USA*. Charles E.
Brooks puts his faith in fishing
a *floating* minnow, giving the
impression that it is dead or
wounded. A closed-cell foam in
any of these minnow streamers
will achieve this.
7 Split Partridge & Red –
New Zealand. Quill feather,
instead of hackle, adapted to
Matuka-style tying. Extremely
effective style.
8 Red Shiner – *Japan*.
Modern tying with Mylar
tinsel.

**1 Giant Gold Stonefly
Larva** – *USA*. Also loosely
termed water cricket. Natural
is *Acroneuria californica*, one
of the most important western
stoneflies. ¾ view.
2 Rassler – *UK*. Update on
Rasputin. Muddler-style head
to increase resemblance to
small baitfish-like bullhead.
3 Cream Sedge Pupa – *UK*.
The standard UK tying. Also
widely available in the other
usual sedge pupa colours.
4 Cream Nymph – *USA*. In
late June and July the upwing
Potamanthus distinctus
hatches. Nymphs about ⅝ inch.
**5 Richard Walker Mayfly
Nymph** – *UK*. Initially tied
with double thorax, and extra
"throat" hackle tied halfway

down the thorax. Weighted.
6 Mayfly Nymphe – *France*.
Nylon legs rather than cock
pheasant tail fibre, otherwise
similar to previous pattern.
7 Orvis All-purpose Light –
USA. Orvis simplified
problems of upwing nymphs
by listing All-purpose Dark,
Medium and Light.
8 Parmachene Belle – *USA*.
Exceptional worldwide as a
fancy pattern, also catching
fish not normally considered
game for the fly rod.
**9 Special White & Silver
Muddler** – *UK*. A long way
from the original **Muddler
Minnow** of Don Gapen.
Variations limitless.
10 Gollidoll – *Kenya*. Original
patterns called **Baby Doll**.

1 Hanningfield Lure – *UK*.
A tandem for the good
rainbows and browns of this
East Anglian stillwater. A
surprisingly effective catcher
of perch.
2 Summer's Gold – *USA/
Canada*. On the Ray Bergman
list in *Trout* as a good fly for
landlocks, lake trout, char,
etc. Tied in miniature.
3 Appetizer – *UK*. This is a
variation of a White Marabou.
Bob Church formulated this
tying, therefore many people
use it.
4 Jack Frost – *UK*. Another
Bob Church pattern.
Fluorescent red tail and
fluorescent white wool used
under clear polythene for the
body distinguish it from the

standard White Marabou.
5 Missionary – *UK*. A fly
with an international history
of development. One of the
first minnow-style imitations
devised in Britain for fishing
Blagdon Reservoir, its
potential was further realized
in New Zealand.
6 Mini Jack Frost – *UK*.
The generations of trout
fishermen brought up on
reservoirs may never have
been introduced to the
traditional loch-style patterns.
If they need small flies they
use scaled-down tyings of
streamers and lures.
7 Barafu – *Kenya*. Variation
of *Jack Frost*, White
Marabou, etc. Weighted,
upside down.

1 Sinfoil's Fry – *UK*. Kent fishery bailiff Ken Sinfoil devised this pattern as a specific imitation of small coarse fish fry on his reservoir. He likes a slender fish-shaped body, using overlay of polythene and mallard or teal flank feather for the wing. "Eye" is optional.

2 Royal Coachman Bucktail – *USA*. One of the most popular American flies in its multiplicity of tying styles.

3 Polystickle – *UK*. The name is made up of Poly for the polythene materials in the dressing and Stickle for stickleback, the small bait fish that the fly imitates.

4 Yorks Kennebago – *USA/ Canada*. Landlocked streamer

recommended by Bergman. Also for lake trout. Up to $4\frac{1}{2}$ inches.

5 Taupo Tiger (Red) – *New Zealand*. Also **Taupo Tiger** (Yellow). A consistently good catcher of trout for more than 40 years.

6 Light Spruce – *USA/ Canada*. Also **Dark Spruce**. Original pattern: couple of turns of red tip, not half body red.

7 Planter – *Kenya*. A number of styles: muddler head, marabou wing, **Jack Frost**-type colouring, extra weight and inversion.

8 White Wonderbug – *UK*. The nymph or pupal shape taken to extremes. Weighted, choice of colours.

1 Brown & White – *USA*.
Typical simple bucktail. Used
for char and landlocked
salmon as well. See also **Red
Shiner**.
2 Nailer – *UK*. Also tied: hair
wing with red fibres under
brown. UK lure Ruby is
similar. Hair-winged version is
possibly more commonly
available.
3 Mary Ann – *USA/Canada*.
Char and landlocked salmon
streamer, tied smaller for the
illustration.
4 Alexis – *Kenya*. Derivation
of traditional **Alexandra**.
Weighted, upside down.
5 Guardsman – *Africa*. Tying
includes golden pheasant crest
over partridge whole feather
wings.

6 Red Dorothy – *New
Zealand*. The Red Dorothy is
possibly the best of the three –
Red, Yellow, or Silver. More
highly favoured are the
Parsons or **Taupo Tiger**.
7 Mother-in-law – *Africa*. A
design by Colonel Unwin's son
Barry. Weighted, upside
down. Illustration shows the
hackling projecting at the
sides and "plated" top
perspective.
8 Hall's Nighttime – *New
Zealand*. Very much a
localized pattern, a design by
Rotorua's Dave Hall, favoured
by those who fish the mouths
of the Rotorua streams.

1 Prince Charlie – *Scotland*.
Compare with Mallard &
Claret, **Grouse & Claret**, etc.
2 Blood Fly – *UK*. Known as
Bloody Mary if tied with
bronze peacock herl body and
dyed red cuckoo hackle.
3 Carter's Pink Lady –
Africa.
4 Corrie Fly – *Scotland*.
5 Adjutant – *Scotland*. Similar
to **Mallard & Claret** and
Grouse & Claret.
Distinguished from Adjutant
Blue – an iron-blue dun
imitation using adjutant stork
feathers.
6 Royal Coachman – *USA*.
Possibly the most popular of
American patterns, although
not a specific imitation in any
of its styles.

7 Cardinal – *USA*. The only
thing in nature that this could
possibly resemble is the bird of
the same name and colour.
However, it is a traditional US
fancy pattern.
8 Montreal – *USA*. Standard
wet fly. Silver Montreal
sometimes listed. For
steelhead – brown bucktail
wing.
9 Woodcock & Mixed – *UK*.
One of a Woodcock & . . .
series, standard and effective
loch trout and sea-trout
traditional patterns. This
example of ''mixed'' shows
half yellow and half red wool.
10 Silver Knight – *Africa*.
Body similar to **Peter Ross**,
but teal wing changed.

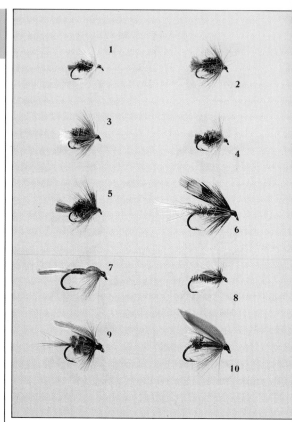

1 Sturdy's Fancy – *UK*. A
grayling fly demonstrating the
common style of many
grayling patterns – sparse
hackle, herl body and brightly
coloured tag.
2 Red Tag – *UK*. Pre-
eminently a grayling fly, it is
also surprisingly useful for
trout all over the world. The
red tag may be either wool or
dyed feather.
3 Treacle Parkin – *UK*. Tied
with yellow tag. Similar to, but
smaller than *Eric's Beetle*.
4 Grayling Witch – *UK*.
Originally dressed palmer-
style, the tyings now have
throat hackles, either light
honey dun or white. German
pattern – Hexe.
5 Bradshaw's Fancy – *UK*.

Probably the most celebrated
invention of Mr Henry
Bradshaw, and an excellent
grayling fly.
6 Vi-Menn Flua – *Norway/*
Denmark/Sweden.
7 Red Nymph – *New*
Zealand. In New Zealand, as
elsewhere, there is a Red
Spinner. Sooner or later wet
flies and nymphs evolve as
tyings of what were originally
dry flies.
8 Emerging Buzzer (Claret)
– *UK*. In many colours.
9 Pomahaka Red – *New*
Zealand. "Companion" to the
Pomahaka Black.
10 Red Ant – *Australia/*
Tasmania. For termites, ant
patterns should have double
the length of wing.

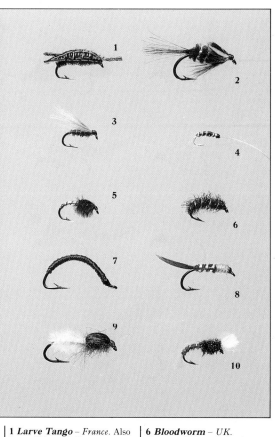

1 *Larve Tango* – *France*. Also Larve Citron, Paille, ***Abricot***, Amande and Parme. Ragot patterns.
2 *Walker's Red Nymph* – *Africa*. Many of the Lionel Walker patterns include partridge wing/thorax/hackle.
3 *Rouge* – *France*. Hackle-point wings.
4 *Camole No 1* – *Italy*. Tied on eye-less hook. Worth considering as a style for tying bloodworm-type flies. The Camole series has quite a reputation for grayling.
5 *Red & Silver Nymph* – *UK*. Also wide series: . . . & Silver Nymph – Black, Green, Pink, White, Pink & Green, Orange & Green. (Knight patterns).

6 *Bloodworm* – *UK*. Chironomid larva imitation. Sparkle from seal's fur gives the illusion of translucence.
7 *Bloodworm* – *Universal*. Many variations on a difficult theme to imitate a chironomid larva.
8 *Red Larva* – *UK*. Also Green Larva in same style.
9 *Persuader* – *UK*. John Goddard tying in a typical nymph/sedge pupa profile to catch the trout's eye rather than imitate nature.
10 *Hatching Red Buzzer* – *UK*. Standard pupa style: cilia at head.

1 *Ginger Mick* (Yellow) – *New Zealand*. Either wool or chenille body. Paler ***Parsons' Glory*** seems to be more popular. Also ***Ginger Mick*** (Red) and (Green).

2 *Matuka* – *Germany*. A very different interpretation of matuka style, with tufts of feather introduced dorsally, rather than hackles tied down with the ribbing.

3 *Taupo Tiger* (Yellow) – *New Zealand*. Also ***Taupo Tiger*** (Red).

4 *Parsons' Glory* (Yellow) – *New Zealand*. Designed by Phil Parsons, probably the most popular of the daytime lures. The honey-barred hackle approximates markings of immature fish. Also lime green.

5 *Rabbit* (Yellow) – *New Zealand*. Inventor possibly Gawen Kenway. Huge variety of body colours, including tinsels. Black Rabbit may be tied with black rabbit skin strip or black cat skin.

6 *Yellow Peril* – *Australia/ Tasmania*. A style within the matuka style; also Red, Tiger and Green. "Longtail" variation with extended dressing behind the hook.

7 *Perch Fry* – *UK*. Variations include: gold tinsel body, with brown and white marabou wing; gold body with wing of yellowish green, dyed grizzle hackles with two light grey hackles on each side, together with orange cock throat hackle.

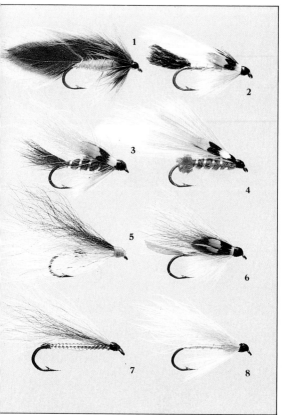

1 Yellow Matuka – *New Zealand*. Note the furnace wing/tail rather than yellow hackle. Original tying included bittern feather (matuku) but its use is now banned. Hen pheasant may be used.
2 Dr Burke – *USA/Canada*. Tied small for the illustration. Streamer for char, landlocked salmon, steelhead, etc.
3 Scott Special – *USA/Canada*. Tied small for the illustration as are the next four patterns. Streamer for landlocked salmon, char, steelhead, etc.
4 Fraser – *USA/Canada*. A 1928 design by Andrew Fraser of the Matapedia.
5 Capra Streamer – *USA/Canada*. A Bergman

recommendation for char, landlocks, etc.
6 Jean – *USA/Canada*. Also a steelhead pattern.
7 Mickey Finn – *USA/general*. Modern tyings use mylar tinsel with its fish-scale effect. Older tyings used flat tinsel. Widespread in use for all game fish. Tied in a variety of sizes, including tandem streamers. Gaining itself a reputation for UK reservoir trout. Came into prominence in the 1930s. Dyed throat hackle optional.
8 Mrs Palmer – *UK*. Richard Walker pattern. The original was tied with extra long yellow goat hair for its extreme mobility and flexibility.

1 *Tanager* –*Africa*. From
John Veniard's listing.
2 *Brown & Scarlet* – *USA/
Canada*. This is a Bergman-
listed streamer appropriate for
landlocked salmon, char and
steelhead. It is tied small for
the illustration.
3 *Matuka Muddler Minnow*
– *New Zealand*. This combines
traditional New Zealand
matuka style with imported
muddler style from the USA.
It has plenty of bulk to give a
good representation of the
cock-a-bully *Gobio morphus*
spp.
4 *Muddler Hopper* –
Australia. When there is a
shortage of upwings, trout
take a greater proportion of
terrestrials.

5 *Texas Rose Muddler* –
UK. This is attributed to
Richard Walker. It is a
variant of the muddler style.
6 *Surface Stonefly* – *USA*.
Should be fished with low
profile in the surface film. Lee
Wulff recommends side casting
with his patented yellow
plastic combination patterns.
7 *Light Mossback* – *USA*.
Extremely robust style of
tying. Effective stonefly or
water beetle larva imitation.
8 *Light Mossback* (special
tying) – *USA*. This is woven
on a special nymph hook in
order to give it melon-seed
breadth.

1 **Breathing Nymph** –
Germany. Tied so that the
fibres project sideways from
the abdomen. Style copied in
alder larvae.
2 **Little Yellow** – *USA*. A
good representation of the
⅓-inch *Isoperla bilineata* or
of *I. marmona*.
3 **Swannundaze Stone** –
USA. Rear body segmented
with broad oval nylon
Swannundaze material.
Weighted.
4 **Perla** – *USA*. Stonefly larva
or nymph. Tied with plenty of
bulk, and weighted. There are
yellow-orange variations in the
Alloperla or *Isoperla* groupings.
5 **Amber Latex Sedge Pupa**
– *UK*.

6 **Gacke Nymph** – *Germany*.
Yugoslav river of this name,
but many patterns shared in
Germany, Austria and
Yugoslavia.
7 **Tellico** – *USA*. Weighted.
Variations include grey turkey
wing cases/back.
8 **Walker's Yellow Nymph** –
Africa. Lionel Walker helped
John Veniard in his list of
modern fly designs for Africa.
9 **Larve Abricot** – *France*.
Interesting contrast with
Mossback. Larve Citron,
Tango, Paille, etc., in this
style.
10 **Green Drake Nymph** –
USA. *Ephemera guttulata*.
Known by many names: shad
fly, mayfly, green may and
green drake.

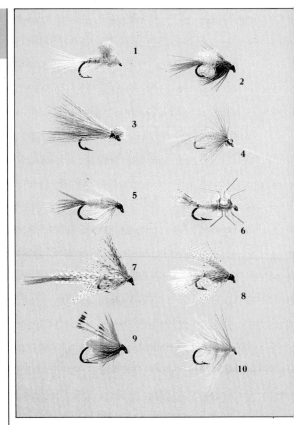

1 Yellow Floating Nymph –
USA. Should float just in the
surface film. Some patterns
include a closed-cell foam
bubble above the thorax.
2 Rekord Nymphe –
Germany.
3 Aufsteiger – *Germany*. Tied
with strands of deer hair.
Stubs left part trimmed
constitute head.
4 Camole No 11 – *Italy*.
Bead eye usual on the Camole
series. Many are highly
recommended for grayling as
well.
5 Half Stone Nymph – *New
Zealand*. Originated as a
hackled fly in Devonshire.
Tied here in nymph style.
6 Yellow May Nymph – *UK*.
From the Burgess catalogue.

French nymph styles
extremely similar.
7 Andelle – *France/Germany*.
See also **Levrière** for
similarity.
8 Preska Nymphe –
Germany.
9 Grasshopper O'Brien's –
Australia/Tasmania. One of
the many hopper imitations.
More to be seen in the dry fly
section.
10 Stewart's Yellow Sally –
UK. A small stonefly with
four thin rolled wings above
the body. Found in abundance
on many rivers from June to
August in the Midlands,
Yorkshire and Wales. Also a
dry pattern. Style with half-
palmered hackle.

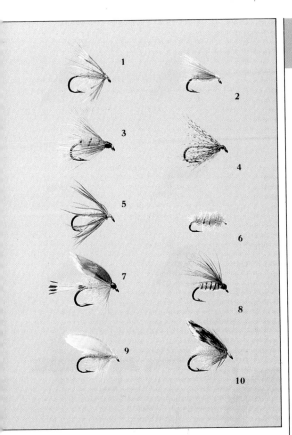

1 Poult Bloa – *UK*. Standard
northern wet pattern to
imitate the pale watery or
nymph of the blue-winged
olive.
2 Jaune – *France*. Also
Rouge and Marron in this
style.
3 Caddis No 1 – *Italy*. Caddis
No 0 and No 2 are of this style
but with very pale grey and
pale grey bodies, respectively.
No 9 is half pale grey and half
brown-bodied.
4 Light Partridge & Yellow
– *UK*. Grey feathers from the
English partridge used for
Light patterns, and brown
feathers for the Dark patterns.
5 Snipe & Yellow – *UK*.
Hackle taken from the
underside of the snipe's wing.

Coarse hackle for plenty of
mobility. Also **Snipe &
Purple** and Snipe & Orange.
6 Jay's Grub – *Japan*.
Thickly wound, and then
trimmed, seal's fur body.
7 Woodcock & Yellow – *UK*.
One of the Woodcock & . . .
series. See **Woodcock &
Green, Woodcock & Mixed**.
8 Palaretta Jaune – *France/
Germany*. Also **Palaretta
Grün**, borrowed in principle
from the French.
9 Yellow Sally – *UK*. One of
the stonefly/needlefly
grouping, *Chloroperla
grammatica*.
10 Greyhen & Yellow –
Scotland/UK. Again a series,
but not as widespread as Teal,
Grouse or Mallard series.

1 Hamill's Variable –
Ireland. Wet mayfly pattern.
Passing resemblance to New
Zealand pattern, **Hamill's
Killer** with the yellow body.
2 Sylph – *Scotland/UK*.
Similar to salmon fly of the
same name or called Gold
Sylph.
3 Kemp – *Africa*. Most sales
of trout flies in Africa are
trout/sea-trout standards.
Extra attractions added in
local tying developments.
4 Californian Coachman –
USA. Substitute the natural
red hackle for dyed yellow,
and the red centre body
section also for yellow, and the
Royal Coachman becomes
the Californian.
5 McGinty – *USA*. A "fancy"

wet fly within the US
tradition with a passing
resemblance to a wasp. Tied
also with a brown and white
bucktail wing.
6 Keeler – *New Zealand*.
Particularly favoured in the
larger sizes. Named after a
lady who caught the "news".
7 Whisky Fly – *UK*.
Although it takes brown trout
well enough, the Whisky Fly
has become notable for its
ability to take rainbows. It is
surprisingly effective when
schooling rainbows are feeding
on daphnia (water fleas).
8 Jersey Herd – *UK*. Body
tinsel should be *bronze*, not
gold, which is sometimes
substituted. The fly should be
fished slowly.

1 Baby Doll (Orange
Fluorescent) – *UK*. One of the
series of Baby Doll patterns;
also Green, White, Scarlet.
Like many other minnow-style
artificials, is best fished not
too fast. Baby Dolls are now
classic reservoir patterns for
rainbow and brown trout.
2 Orange Muddler – *USA/
general*. There is one original
Muddler Minnow pattern. This
is a simple derivation with
dyed orange fibres taking the
place of the oak turkey trail,
grey squirrel hair and oak
turkey wing.
3 Frog Nobbler – *UK*. Bob
Church established an
alternative to some of the
other lead-headed jigs by a
series of this name. Colours:

orange, blue, green, yellow,
etc. Bodies: silver, gold, as
well as colours.
4 Ted's Stone – *USA*.
Chenille, with its water
absorption and strong colour,
is a feature of this stonefly
imitation, which is a variation
of the standard **Montana**.
5 Church Fry – *UK*. A Bob
Church design. The
combination of orange, a
colour attractive to rainbows,
and its mobile squirrel hair
wing, makes it deservedly
popular.
6 Geronimo – *UK*. Despite
its name, only its style comes
from the USA; a Brian Harris
pattern. Variation: furnace
hackles for the wing instead of
the standard cree hackles.

1 Plucker – *Kenya*. Variation on Muddler theme, with Mylar body, weighted and upside down.

2 Alder Larva – *UK*. Voracious larva of a blackish/brownish adult fly (*Sialis lutaria*). Middle of May to middle of June. Female larger than the male. Usually fished slow and well sunk. The gills line the sides of the abdomen and are normally emphasised in artificials.

3 Fruit Salad – *New Zealand*. The New Zealand equivalent of the UK moorhen is the longer-legged, blue-sheen-feathered pukeko, whose plumage appears to be valuable for fly tying.

4 Latex Prawn – *Japan*.

Compare with salmon flies resembling shrimps and prawns. This is somewhat similar to the Riding brothers' latex prawn.

5 Mountain Swallow – *Africa*. A fancy pattern tied to resemble in general colour the bird known as the bee-eater.

6 Beastie – *UK*. Weighted head to give diving dipping motion on an irregularly paced retrieve. Forerunner of Nobbler, **Frog Nobbler**-type developments. Marabou sleeks down to give vibrant mobile effect. A Geoffrey Bucknall concept. In many colours.

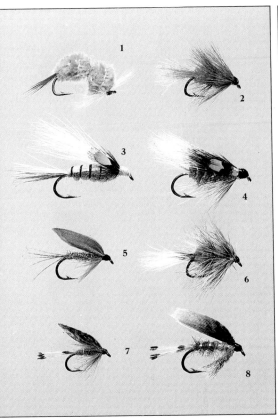

1 Salmon Egg – *Italy*. If they work for steelhead, there is no reason why they should not work for resident rainbows. Tied also as a single egg.
2 Red Setter – *New Zealand*. A style like that of the *Fuzzy Wuzzy*. Variation has wool body and black tail. Another Geoff Sanderson pattern. Renowned for taking lake-run trout, particularly after dark. Its make-up has a vague resemblance to the koura, a freshwater crayfish.
3 Orange Streamer – *USA/ Canada*. Tied small for the illustration. For landlocked salmon, char, steelhead, etc.
4 Macgregor – *USA/Canada*. Tied small for the illustration. Streamer for landlocked salmon, char, steelhead, etc.
5 Orange Germ – *Scotland*. Blae-type wing.
6 Dappled Dog (Orange) – *New Zealand*. Also Green Fluorescent. These patterns should be tied with fluorescent body materials. Initially the fly was introduced on the Tongario. Since then it has scored well elsewhere.
7 Grouse & Orange – *Scotland/UK*. One of the Grouse series. Also for sea-trout in larger sizes.
8 African Belle – *Africa*. Very similar to sea-trout Turkey & Mixed, and to trout **Woodcock & Mixed** (in smaller sizes and lesser styles).

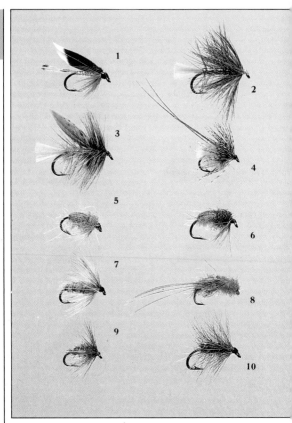

1 Rector's Fancy – *Africa*.
Similar to **Heckham
Peckham** or **Bloody
Butcher**.
2 Orange & Gold – *UK*. Tied
bob-style. A palmered pattern.
3 Orange Sedge – *UK*. Tied
bushy for surface work.
4 Amber Longhorn – *UK*.
Richard Walker development.
Body alternatively of
lambswool or seal's fur. Also
Green Longhorn.
5 Amber Nymph (Small) –
UK. Designed by Dr Howard
Bell for fishing at Blagdon in
the early part of the century.
Successful sedge pupa
imitation.
6 Amber Nymph (Large) –
UK. Companion to **Amber
Nymph** (Small) from the

same originations.
7 Bread Crust – *USA*.
Nymph representing a broad
spectrum of subaquatic life.
8 Orange Sedge Pupa – *UK*.
Another style of sedge pupa
dressing. Also Brown, Green,
Cream, etc.
9 Grenadier – *UK*. Another
Dr Bell pattern devised for
Blagdon; now general. Can be
dressed bushy as a bob-fly, or
even dry. Resembles certain
small beetles, moths or sedges.
Tied as a nymph.
10 Soldier Palmer – *UK*.
More fully palmer-hackled
than the **Grenadier**. Fly of
considerable antiquity as the
Red Palmer. May have red tag
added. Tied more heavily as a
bob-fly.

1 Spider No 2 – *Italy*. The hackles must be tied facing forwards to give the style its "kick" under water.
2 Camole No 30 – *Italy*. Some of the series use cock hackle instead of partridge or other coarse-fibre hackle. Colour range is extremely diverse.
3 Stewart's Woodcock & Orange – *UK*. Stewart, a Scottish angler, fished his mobile wet flies upstream, precursors of modern nymph designs.
4 Chomper (Orange) – *UK*. Shrimp-like modern pattern from Goddard. If weighted, weight should lie along the back, allowing it to swim upside down.

5 Pond Olive Nymphe – *France*. Markedly pinker than a name olive would suggest. Also within this French style: Autumn Dun Nymphe and Large Brooke Nymphe.
6 Shrimper (Orange) – *UK*. Wide colour range through olives, beiges and greys.
7 Blue Quill Nymph – *USA*. Illustrated here because so surprisingly amber in colour for such a pattern name. Dry patterns: Gordon Quill, etc.
8 Bachflokrebs – *Germany*. Weighted crustacean imitation.
9 Nymph Typ C – *Germany*.
10 Duck Fly – *Ireland*. Irish designation of chironomid or midge, or buzzer. Wide range of colours.

1 Black Ant – *USA*. Centre-hackled: winged patterns alternative. See also **Red Ant**, **Red Flying Ant**, etc.

2 Black Flying Ant – *USA*. Deer hair incorporated plus "iridescent" wing. View from above.

3 Black Ant – *UK*. Body material in hourglass shape, with hackle at shoulders. Also **Red Ant**, or any other appropriate colour.

4 Flying Ant – *General*. Legs heavily emphasized.

5 Black Ant (balsa) – *USA*. For similar effect, use closed-cell foam, and varnish it black.

6 Black Gnat – *UK*. *Bibio johannis* is the basic insect, but *Simulium* sp and other

small black aquatics or terrestrials are copied by Black Gnats.

7 Halford's Black Gnat – *UK*. Slender body, wings sloping back. Although devised about 80 years ago, still seems a reliable tying.

8 No-hackle Black Gnat – *Italy*. A style that depends on well splayed tail fibres. *Bibio* does not have a tail!

9 Black Gnat – *New Zealand*. Probably taken as a blowfly imitation. Dean's Black Gnat has silver rib.

10 Black Gnat Parachute – *USA*. Black gnats in America are *Diptera*, as are some of the UK examples, but basically *Hilara*, particularly *H. femorata*.

1 Black Spider – *New Zealand*. Sometimes "spider" means a slight tying, or a very long hackled tying for the size of hook.

2 Blue Bottle – *Norway/ Denmark/Sweden*. Terrestrial imitation. See also wet patterns.

3 Knotted Midge – *Ireland*. One way to represent a small insect is to tie two at once on the same hook. It floats better and makes a more enticing mouthful.

4 Black Spinner – *Australia/ Tasmania*. Represents the spinners of some upwings. The natural is the male imago of the river march brown.

5 Black Angel – *Japan*. Departure from US Black Angel tying, which has black hackle tip wings and black floss body.

6 Hawthorne – *UK*. Bibio marci, larger relative of the black gnat, with trailing legs.

7 Black Skater – *Norway/ Denmark/Sweden*. Should float well on hackle tips without dragging.

8 Demon – *Norway/Denmark/ Sweden*. Silver tinsel body.

9 Black Spider – *UK*. Very slender, sparse, long hackle, no wing. Black gnat or midge general pattern, particularly when tied with off-black body.

10 Silver Tail – *Norway/ Denmark/Sweden*. Also silver tinsel body.

1 D 10 – *Switzerland*. Hackle points for wings – an element of translucency and extreme delicacy of tying.

2 Black Midge – *USA*. Midge is a term for the truly diminutive. A number of dressings are regularly tied this small as a style.

3 Black Crowe Beetle – *USA*. Terrestrial: one of the styles evolved with the use of deer hair. Bulk, buoyancy and legs all from one material.

4 Ti-tree Beetle – *Australia/ Tasmania*. Full shoulder hackle to help it float. There are two sorts, the black and brown, and the green and yellow.

5 Black Beetle – *USA*. Another beetle style: peacock herl body, black palmered, and wing cases tied in fore and aft.

6 Black Buzzer Adult – *UK*. Trout seek adults that are sunken or awash.

7 Sedge Noire – *France*. A number of black sedges are found generally in Europe: *Athripsodes nigronervosus* and *Silo nigricornis*, and the black silverhorns, *Mystacides azurea* or *M. nigra* or *Athripsodes atterimus*.

8 Alder – *UK*. The natural is *Sialis liatris* in the UK, and its larva is an aquatic insect important in trout diet.

9 Black Sedge – *UK*. The natural black sedges are indicated above.

10 Black Sedge – *Italy*.

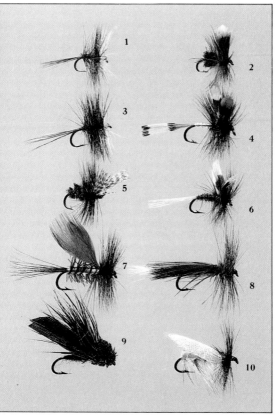

1 Macquarie Black –
Australia/Tasmania. White
shoulder hackle added as an
aid to visibility. An
alternative to the **Black
Spinner**.
2 Green Devil – *Japan*.
3 Black Bivisible – *USA*.
Another of the Hewitt
patterns. Rides high and floats
well in rough, fast streams.
4 Jungle Cock (Silver) –
Norway/Denmark/Sweden. Tied
as a standard wet pattern as
well. Indicative of the
popularity of jungle cock in
Scandinavian tyings.
5 John Storey – *UK*. Tied
here extremely dark. Forward
winging is a relatively modern
development in this pattern.
Usually tied with dark natural

red hackle.
6 Black Eagle – *Japan*.
White tips to wings to aid
visibility.
7 Nattvakten – *Norway/
Denmark/Sweden*.
8 Nattslåndan – *Norway/
Denmark/Sweden*. A dark
sedge or stonefly imitation.
9 Letort Cricket – *USA*. Tied
for particularly selective trout
in the Letort in Pennsylvania.
Development of pattern by
Ernest Schwiebert, Edward
Shank and Edward Koch. In
1962, during its trials, it
accounted for a 9-lb trout.
10 Resting Sedge – *Germany*.
An example of artificial
winging material – a fine
woven nylon.

1 Olive Dun – *UK*. Some of the most widespread of the upwings are the *Baëtis* spp. "Duns" usually have dubbed bodies, "Quills" have stripped peacock quills, "Rough" have coarser seal's fur body.
2 Blue-Winged Olive Thorax – *USA*. This name is normally applied to *Baëtis* spp of the USA. Variety of winging material available.
3 Rough Olive – *UK*. Good general olive pattern, decreasing in size and tone as the season progresses.
4 Large Dark Olive – *UK*. About as dark green as any tyings go. Female imago is imitated by **Red Spinner**.
5 Pale Watery – *UK*. Four naturals, all practically identical, are represented by the Pale Watery.
6 Large Spurwing Dun – *UK*. An upside down tying of a cutwing style.
7 D 2 – *Switzerland*. Hackle point wings instead of quill.
8 Hatching Olive – *UK*. Extra emphasis on the thorax. Rather a higher-riding emerger than some of the US Swisher and Richards designs.
9 Medium Olive (No-hackle) – *Italy*. Adoption of a US style. Depends largely on well spread tails to help it land balanced and float. $\frac{3}{4}$ view.
10 Olive Midge – *USA*. Diminutive style. Possibly imitating aphids or anything else extremely small and greenish.

1 Green Adult Buzzer – *UK.*
Alternatives are the
traditional series patterns:
Grouse & Green, Mallard &
Green, Woodcock & Green,
etc. Chironomid imitation; fish
either in the surface film or
just under.
2 Inchworm – *USA.* Imitates
the small green caterpillar that
hazardously swings on a
thread and occasionally falls
into the water. Because the
style is not hackled it is tied
from buoyant materials.
3 Green Stonefly – *New
Zealand.* The adult *Stenoperla
prasina* is imitated with green-
bodied tyings, as is its larva.
4 Cicada – *New Zealand.*
Large palmered flies of the
matching colours are often

used. This is more specific.
5 Green Peter – *Ireland.*
Peter is the sedge, huge and
speckled, hatching at dusk in
late July and early August.
Experienced Irish fishers use it
all season.
6 Olive Caddis – *USA.* Gary
LaFontaine in *Caddis Flies*
recommends deerhair caddis
adults as good searching
patterns. Many colours.
7 Goddard & Henry Sedge
(Green) – *UK.* Also Orange.
Stripped hackle stalk antennae
prevent nosediving. Clipped
deer hair gives shape and
buoyancy. Green or orange
seal's fur belly.
8 Dunkelgrüne Sedge –
Germany. Very low profile.

91

1 Maifliege Grau-Olive –
Germany. Europe has two
common mayflies: *Ephemera
danica* and *E. vulgata.* These
large upwings are important
because they bring large trout
to the feed.

2 Hackle Mayfly – *UK.*
Rather than use fan wings, the
shoulder hackle (dyed gallina)
gives a wing impression.
Palmer hackle ensures high
riding qualities.

3 Citron May – *France.* Pale
yellowish French tying.

4 French Partridge Mayfly
– *UK.* The flank feathers of
French partridge *Alectoris rufa*
are used at the shoulder. Not
a pattern from France!

5 Green Mayfly – *USA.* The
natural *Ephemera guttulata* has

the same importance in the
USA as *E. danica* and *E.
vulgata* in Europe, with a wide
variety of patterns. Tail fibres
of hair are probably more
successful than cock pheasant
tail fibres.

6 Gray Wulff – *USA.*
Ephemera guttulata imitation
in its home country, and *E.
danica* when exported to
Britain, where it is often tied
with the wing projecting well
forward, and *not* split.

7 Green Drake Wulff – *USA.*

8 Green Mayfly – *USA.*
Another *Ephemera guttulata*
tying.

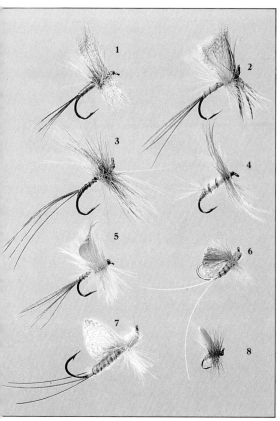

1 Fanwing Grizzly King –
USA. Grizzly King tied also as
a standard trout wet, and in
appropriate style, steelhead fly
and as a streamer.
2 Halford Green Male –
France. Halford was <u>the</u>
codifier of dry fly fishing for
trout, based on chalkstreams
in southern England. His
books were adopted widely
throughout trout fishing
countries.
3 Pale May Female Dun –
UK. This is a dyed poultry
hackle version, with strong
dyed red incorporated. Since
1900 strong "unnatural"
colours have proved quite an
attraction.
4 Tannlegen – *Norway/
Denmark/Sweden.*

5 Raphia – *France.* Silk when
wet or oiled grows darker.
Dubbing or fur can become
saturated. Most countries use
materials such as raffia in
both sub-imago and imago
patterns.
6 Autumn Dun – *UK.* Upside
down cutwing style. Natural is
Ecdyonurus dispar. The
common name, now
superseded, was august dun.
7 Mayfly Dun (Female) –
UK.
8 Yellow Sally – *UK.* The
natural is *Chloroperla
grammatica,* a small stonefly.

1 Ballhead Hopper – *USA.*
Deer hair is used here to
provide extra buoyancy and
bulk. The partly "detached"
body is of twisted wool. If the
pattern is to be finished wet,
the body is not as buoyant as
patterns tied with muddler-
style clipped body.

2 Grasshopper – *USA.*
Addition of knotted turkey
quill legs. There is a muddler-
style head and thick cream
wool body, palmer hackled
natural red.

3 Dad's Demoiselle – *UK/*
general. This is patterned to
represent the common blue
damsel fly. The same style and
tying can be employed for a
number of other coloured
insects.

4 Deer Hopper – *USA.* This
is a combination of previous
hopper styles.

5 Silver Doctor – *Norway/*
Denmark/Sweden. Very few
dyed blue dry flies. Normally
natural blues are used, and
insects are directly imitated.

6 Whit's Spent Damsel –
USA. Dave Whitlock's
approach to this tying
problem. Eyes are glued on.
Other colour possibilities are
left to the tier's taste. It is
tied spinner-style, resembling
an exhausted adult.

7 Damsel Fly – *USA.* The
fore and aft hackles will give a
confused footprint, but this
looks a less convincing style
than the previous patterns.

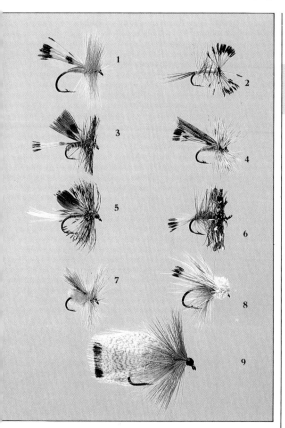

1 Wilson's Hopper –
Australia/Tasmania. The usual
grasshoppers have a yellow
body and black and orange
legs. A whole range of
imitations follows. The hopper
season lasts through
December, January, February
and March, and the insects
increase in size as they grow
older.
2 Hackle Hopper – *Australia/
Tasmania*.
3 Grasshopper – Berchdolt
– *Australia/Tasmania*.
4 Grasshopper – O'Brien's
– *Australia/Tasmania*.
5 Snowy Mountains Hopper
– *Australia/Tasmania*.
6 Kaktus – *Norway/Denmark/
Sweden*.

7 Hopper Glen Innes –
Australia/Tasmania.
8 Nobby Hopper – *Australia/
Tasmania*.
9 Orange Mallard –
Switzerland. The body is made
of black chenille, ribbed gold
oval.

1 Red Flying Ant – *USA*.
When ants land on the water,
trout favour them. A variety
of styles is shown (see also
Black Ant). There are
cinnamon, ginger, etc., as well.
2 Red Ant (Balsa) – *USA*.
Tied with positive buoyancy
material, varnished red.
3 Red Flying Ant
(Fluorescent) – *USA*. Another
style with positive buoyancy;
dyed red deer hair. The wing
is exaggerated in colour.
4 Red Ant (Winged) –
Australia/Tasmania. A more
traditional tying with hackle
forward and hackle point
wings sloping back.
5 Great Lake Beetle –
Australia/Tasmania. There are
fewer upwings available to the

trout, and more terrestrials
form their diet – beetles, ants,
hoppers, etc.
6 Bradshaw's Fancy – *UK*.
Fancy fly for grayling, in
company with **Red Tag**,
Steel Blue, etc., from the
North Country.
7 La Loue – *France*.
8 Red Quill Thorax – *USA*.
Distinct from the UK **Red
Quill**, which is tied with quill.
Locally may be known as
whirling dun.
9 Lake Olive Spinner – *UK*.
Represents adult of *Cloëon
simile*. In all the usual tyings
body is reddish.
**10 Blue-Winged Olive
Spinner** – *UK*. One of the
most widespread upwings in ·
the UK. Adult form tying.

1 Orange/Silver Adult Dry Midge – *UK*. In the same style and in smaller sizes: Brown, Red, Black, Cream, etc.

2 Red Adult Midge – *UK*. Another style; also colours as appropriate.

3 Parachute Buzzer – *UK*. Small vertical fluorescent wing stub with no real representation of the natural wing set of chironomids. Helps the angler see his fly as he fishes.

4 Sherry Spinner (Upside Down) – *UK*. Traditional representation of the spinner of the blue-winged olive *Ephemerella ignita*. Upside down, with spread hackle-point wings.

5 Burrinjuck Wonder – *Australia/Tasmania*.

6 Orange Spinner – *Australia/Tasmania*.

7 Ecureil – *France*.

8 Orange John – *UK*. John Ketley pattern for loch-style fishing late in the season. To be bobbed along as a top dropper. Sedge-style.

9 Orange Caddis – *USA*. Hair, usually deer, has replaced feather wings in many caddis imitations. It can be bunched and set at the required angle by varnishing its roots.

10 Soldier Beetle – *UK*. *Telephorus rusticus* according to Courtney Williams. *Cantharis rustica* according to Goddard.

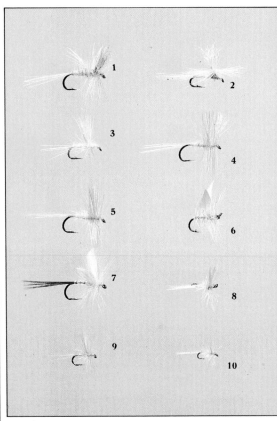

1 Light Cahill – *USA*. See wet.

2 Light Cahill Parachute – *USA*. Another style approach. Hair wing has replaced the original rolled duck wing.

3 Light Cahill Thorax – *USA*. The body should be close to the surface; the hackle, similar to the wing colour, should splay at random at the centre of the fly. The body of the natural being upturned will appear foreshortened from below.

4 Pale Evening Dun – *USA*. Naturals: *Epeorus vitrea*, hatching at twilight in May and June. Also known as pale watery duns or little marryatts.

5 Pale Sulphur Dun – *USA*.

Natural: *Ephemerella dorothea*.

6 White Moth – *UK*. General pale sedge/moth pattern. More modern interpretations use muddler-style tyings, like White Mini Muddler.

7 White Miller – *USA*. Tied wet and dry. Although dressed in upwing style, it is considered to imitate a pale sedge – *Leptocella albida*, and similar species.

8 Caenis (Angler's Curse) – *UK*. Smallest of the upwings and highly favoured by trout.

9 D 1 – *Switzerland*.

10 Cream Midge – *USA*. Styled rather than a directly imitative dressing. Applicable during *Caenis* hatches. Similar to **Last Hope**, **Caenis**, etc.

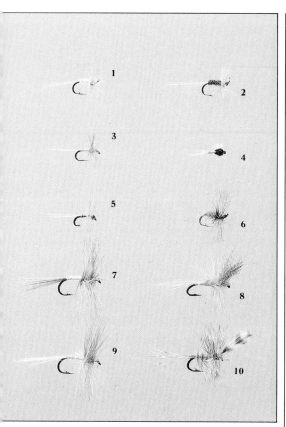

1 Last Hope (Light) – *UK*. John Goddard imitation of the *Caenis* species.
2 Last Hope (Dark) – *UK*. Companion fly to the Light pattern.
3 D 4 – *Switzerland*.
4 Caenis Polywing – *UK*. Shows how infuriatingly small the "angler's curse" is. Trout favour these diminutive morsels, and are very selective.
5 Gloire de Neublans – *France*.
6 Grey Duster – *UK*. Highly recommended by Courtney Williams in *A Dictionary of Trout Flies*, at the early stages of the mayfly hatch. Possibly a representation of the smaller *Perlidae*, or an early olive.

7 Gray Fox Variant – *USA*. Variant style, with longer hackle. Taller, sparser appearance than the standard style. Insects are *Stenonema fuscum*, *S. vicarium* and *S. ithaca*.
8 Light Hendrickson – *USA*. See wet entry.
9 Cream Variant – *USA*. The natural is *Potamanthus*, twilight hatcher on eastern rivers. Local names include golden drake, cream dun, evening dun and golden spinner.
10 Coucou Mole – *France*. Style: Mole, i.e., wings pointing forwards (until we come to a New Zealand Mole pattern). Coucou = hackle colour.

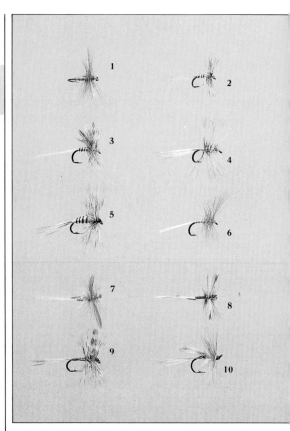

1 Grey-Yellow Spent –
France.
2 Moucheron Chinchilla –
France. According to
Pequegnot in *Pêche à la
mouche en Bretagne*, French
poultry are bred as "coucou"
and as soon as the hackles
reach the fly tier they are
often called chinchilla.
Patterns such as some tyings
of **Assassine** exemplify this.
**3 Moucheron Ailes
Chinchilla** – *France.*
Variation on body with
inclusion of hackle-tip wings.
4 Europa Vire – *France.*
5 Krebserl – *Germany.*
6 Spent Grey – *France.*
7 Imago Grey – *France.*
8 Spent Grey Claire –
France.

9 Mosquito – *USA.* Tied to
imitate mosquitoes and similar
gnats. Surprisingly, has
upwing style of winging. Tied
in truly diminutive sizes,
"midge" style.
10 Moskito – *Norway/
Denmark/Sweden.* In all
fairness these must be the
commonest insects, judging by
my visit to Finland. They
have laid back wings in more
imitative style than the
American pattern.

1 **Spinner Perle** – *France*.
2 **Europa Rouge-Gris** –
France. Widely spaced turns of
three colours of palmer and
throat hackle.
3 **May Dun** – *Switzerland*.
4 **Fiske-Jo** – *Norway/
Denmark/Sweden*.
5 **Spinner Argentée** –
France.
6 **Mill Evening Spinner** –
UK. Pattern from Orvis UK
on their tributary of the Test.
Also Mill Evening Dun, with
upright quill wings.
7 **Hairwing Variant** – *USA*.
Wulff style in combination
with variant style. Strong tail,
forward hair wings, but
outsize hackling to stand the
fly well up on tiptoe. Colour
variations to choice.

8 **Feather Loop Brown
Quill** – *USA*. According to
Schwiebert, André Puyans
must be credited with this
most diaphanous of winging
styles. Tied single or in pairs,
or laid flat as spinner wings.
Hackle here applied parachute
style.
9 **Favourite de Galley** –
France. Coucou or chinchilla
palmer-hackled body.
10 **Jaco Special 110** –
Switzerland. Coarse-fibred
hackle, trimmed, but with
cock hackle point wings.

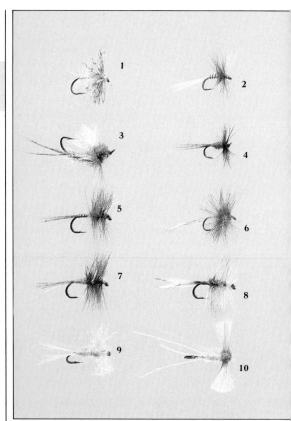

1 Assassine – *Germany/*
France. This is a Pequegnot
tying, a general imitation with
good floating properties – with
the Ragot tackle firm's style
of tying in the palmer hackle.
2 Fibre des Hackles Grise –
France. Note wing tied
forward.
3 Blue Dun Upside-down –
Norway/Denmark/Sweden. In
the past decade there has been
a move towards disguising the
hook from the trout in a
floating fly by turning the fly
upside down. Swedes and
Danes had special hooks made
so that the hackle could be
tied at an angle to the shank.
4 Iron Blue Dun – *UK.* See
wet entry.
5 Quill Gordon – *USA.* Also

Gordon Quill. See wet entry.
6 Erpelfliege Gelb –
Germany. A style from duck-
down type feathers. There are
a number of patterns in this
style.
7 Dark Hendrikson – *USA.*
See also wet pattern.
8 Badger Bivisible – *USA.*
One of the merits of the
badger hackle is that the dark
list is clearly defined and the
white outer fibre not so
obvious to the fish.
**9 Polywing Spinner Green
Drake** – *USA.* Included to
show how little green there is
in this pattern.
10 Broadwing Spinner –
UK. Tied larger than life size.
Hackle fibre wings spread
sideways in tufts.

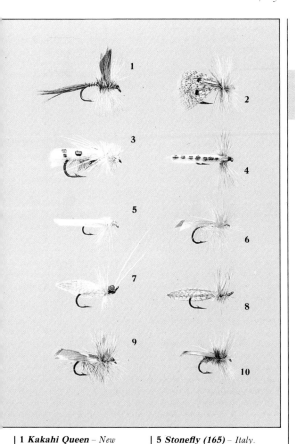

1 Kakahi Queen – *New Zealand*. Developed by Basil Humphries, postmaster at Kakahi. Tied wet and dry to represent probably *Ameletopsis percitus*, a common upwing.

2 Lace Moth – *New Zealand*. Name given to a leaf hopper imitation. The insect has a small body compared with its wing size.

3 Boswell's Moth – *UK*. Muddler influence with muddler buoyancy. A modern update in style and efficacy over dated similar patterns such as Ermine Moth.

4 Stonefly (161) – *Italy*. Where natural materials fail, a waterproof marker pen can produce the wing markings. View from above.

5 Stonefly (165) – *Italy*. Demonstrates long, thin, rolled wing of needlefly type stoneflies. Yellow body.

6 Grey Sedge – *Italy*. Pronounced Vee shape to trailing edge of the wing.

7 Silver Sedge Adult – *UK*. From the Burgess catalogue. Molten nylon eyes are a feature of some of the flies.

8 Silver Sedge – *France*. Similar style, apart from lack of eyes and antennae.

9 Guinea Sedge – *Italy*. Named from choice of winging material, which comes from guinea fowl. Heavily palmered body.

10 Shannon Moth – *Australia/ Tasmania*. A snowflake caddis, *Asmicridea grisea*, imitation.

1 La Favourite – *France*. One of the *La Loue* series.

2 Jaco Special 108 – *Switzerland*.

3 Blue Dun Flying – *Germany*.

4 Blue Quill Flying – *Germany*.

5 Myggen Grey – *Norway/Denmark/Sweden*.

6 Blue Quill – *USA*. American pattern of this name represents *Epeorus pluralis*, also known as gordon quill, grey quill and grey dun. Imitations of those names also used. Tied wet. UK pattern of this name – similar dressing represents *Baëtis* olives and pale wateries *Centroptilum* sp and *Procloëon*. Imitations of these insects range from palest of gingers and creams to greys, natural blues and pale olives.

7 Blue Upright – *UK*. Originally a wet pattern from the West Country. *Baëtis* spp imitation. Should be tied with dark natural blue-grey hackles. Taken for large dark olive, iron blue, willow fly, etc.

8 Dun Variant – *UK*. "This name is generally used to denote nondescript long-hackled dry flies." Any standard can be adapted. This example is not winged.

9 Blue Dun – *UK*. Useful to imitate either dark olives or iron blues. Huge number of regional variations. See page 102.

10 Blue Dun No-hackle – *Italy*.

1 *Blue Upright* – *UK.*
Winged example.
2 *D 3* – *Switzerland.*
3 *Grey Green* – *France.*
4 *Gray Bivisible* – *USA.* The
western seaboard rivers are
turbulent. A dry fly must float
well and visibly. Imitation is
therefore less important. Also
a series: Black, Olive, Brown,
etc. George LaBranche's *The
Dry Fly and Fast Water*
explains their use.
5 *Blue-Winged Olive* –
USA. In America this name is
a general term for many *Baëtis*
and other naturals. One is
Ephemerella attenuata, another
being *E. excrucians*. Blue Quill
Spinner represents the adults.
6 *Jenny Spinner* – *France.*
Represents male adult of iron

blue *Baëtis pumilis* or *B. niger*.
In the UK the male spinner
does not seem to be very
popular with trout. Its
pattern: cream or ivory body,
terminally tipped red.
7 *Badger & Yellow* – *UK.*
One of the series: Badger &
Red, & Orange, & Silver, &
Gold. Contrast with grayling
patterns that use the badger
hackle palmer fashion.
8 *Half Stone* – *UK.*
Debatably a representation of
a hatching nymph.
9 *Roman Moser Dun* –
Germany. Traun River
Products wing material used
in upwing imitation.
10 *Jaco Special 102* –
Switzerland. Coarse fibre
hackle.

1 Spent Black Drake – *UK.* Imago or spinner of *Ephemera vulgata* or *E. danica*, the mayfly. Illustrated from above. Terminology: black drake – male spinner, spent drake, spent gnat – all adults. Green drake is the dun or sub-imago. Gray drake is the female adult spinner. No throat hackle in this pattern.

2 Spent-wing May, raffia body – *UK.* Hackle point wings. Clipped hackle at thorax. Some tiers splay the tails on their spent patterns.

3 White May – *France.* Strongly palmered body to support short mallard flank shoulder hackle.

4 Flyline Mayfly (White) – *UK.* Extended body style.

Stripped hackle stalks for tails, for strength, better than fibres from cock pheasant tail.

5 Halford Mayfly – *France.* Fan-winged, much in the style of the four patterns given by F. M. Halford in his 1910 *Modern Development of the Dry Fly*. Disliked as a style by some fishermen because the fly has bad aerodynamics during casting.

6 Parachute Grise – *France.* Illustrated from above to show set of fan wings.

7 Maifliege Hell Grau – *Germany.* Pale grey tying, with fan wings, which had a vogue in the UK but have since fallen out of fashion.

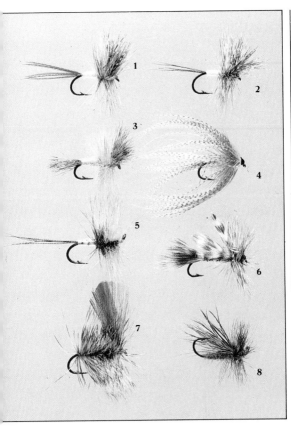

1 Coffin Fly – *USA*. Name given to spinner of *Ephemera guttulata*, the green drake of mid-May to mid-June emergence. Art Flick suggests porcupine quill for the body of his pattern.

2 Grizzly Spinner – *USA*. Name taken from hackle (grizzly), and wing body of spent insect (spinner).

3 Blonde Wulff – *USA*. Lee Wulff pattern of 1920s. The appropriately coloured and sized Wulff patterns have found acceptance in the UK as mayfly imitations, dapping flies, and general pattern bobflies.

4 Gosling – *Ireland/UK*. Style rather than essential tying. Similar to **Straddlebug**.

Fished in the surface film.

5 Yorkshire Mayfly – *UK*. Fairly standard dressing except for addition of fluorescent wings, tied from tufts of artificial fibre.

6 Dragon – *USA*. Since larval forms are very much part of trout diet, it is not unreasonable to produce an adult form.

7 Shadow Mayfly – *UK*. It may not look like the upwing duns we recognize as mayflies but it certainly can have its moment. It floats on the very points of the hackles and can be twitched to give an impression of life.

8 LaFontaine's Dancing Caddis – *USA*. Upside down on Swedish dry-fly hook.

1 Adams – *USA*. Originated by Len Halliday and christened on the river Boardman in 1922. The first tyings had spent wings.

2 Adams Irresistible – *USA*. Clipped wound deerhair body presents a substantial yet buoyant profile in this variation on the standard.

3 Adams Parachute – *USA*. By changing the plane of the hackle, the fly floats on rather than above the surface film. Radiating hackle fibres provide plenty of support but give a different footprint on the water.

4 Adams Thorax – *USA*. Emphasis on balanced presentation. Hackle is set farther back down the body, and the head element enlarged.

5 Adams Midge – *USA*. A miniature of the modern accepted **Adams** standard.

6 Beacon Beige – *UK*. A Peter Deane tying developed from the Beige of 1948. Pattern hugely improved by inclusion of red game cock hackle.

7 Pont Audemer – *France*. Favoured on the Normandy rivers. Tied in a number of variations.

8 Frégate – *France*.

9 Greenwell's Glory – *UK/general*. Compare with other Greenwell's entries.

10 Dark Cahill – *USA*. See wet.

1 Gray Fox *USA*. Natural:
Stenonema fuscum. Nymphs
may head for the shallows before
emerging, which may take
quite some time. Also called
dark gray fox.
2 Lensmannsflua – *Norway/
Denmark/Sweden*.
3 Troutfly – *Germany*.
4 Dark Red Spinner – *New
Zealand*. Probably imitates
one of the *Deleatidium* group of
upwings, the Mataura midge
being the imago.
5 D 8 – *Switzerland*.
6 Spent Olive Noire –
France. France shares many of
the same upwing genera and
species with the UK.
7 Nut Brown Beetle –
Africa. $\frac{3}{4}$ view to show
extending wings and jungle

cock wing cases. Fished in the
surface film or wet.
8 Brown Beetle – *New
Zealand*. Natural: *Odontria*,
about $\frac{1}{2}$ inch long and quite
stocky. **Coch-y-bondhu**
recommended in the beetle
season. Also the tiger beetle,
Nescicindella tuperaulata,
forms part of fish diet.
9 Adult Beige Buzzer – *UK*.
To be fished in the surface
film or just sunk. Imitation of
suitably coloured chironomid.
Wide range of colours
standard.
10 Brown Flying Ant –
USA. For other styles see
Black Ants and **Red Ants**,
wet and dry. The carpenter
ant is somewhat bigger and is
built in three parts.

1 Coch-y-bondhu Bustet – *Norway/Denmark/Sweden*. Palmered variation of standard tying.

2 Coch-y-bondhu Quill – *New Zealand*. Probably taken as an ephemerid imitation. Far from the standard pattern so hardly deserving the Coch-y-bondhu prefix.

3 Twilight Beauty – *New Zealand*. Pattern designed by Basil Humphrey of Kakahi. Dressed dry probably taken as an upwing imitation. The natural spinner of *Coloburiscus humeralis* is also called twilight beauty.

4 Red-tip Governor – *New Zealand*. See wet entry. Probably simulates some beetle. Pattern also seen tied with stripped quill body.

5 D 9 – *Switzerland*.

6 Humla – *Norway/Denmark/Sweden*.

7 Royal Coachman – *USA/general*. Hugely popular: wet, dry, streamer, Wulff-style, for steelhead and salmon as well.

8 Nameless Killer – *New Zealand*. Cream-tipped starling body feathers for wings.

9 Nimmo's Killer – *New Zealand*.

10 Penstock Brown – *Australia/Tasmania*. Natural is *Atalophlebia superba*, also called large brown dun. Cocky Spinner also used.

1 Président Billard – *France*.
A yellow-bodied **Mole Fly**.
Cocks well, and the style
"Mole" is found in other
French patterns, e.g., **Coucou
Mole**, but in that instance
with hackle point wings.
2 Mole Fly – *UK*. Standard
pattern, named after the River
Mole. Floats well, cocks well
and is a good general purpose
fly, in use in almost every
country except the UK.
3 Mole Fly – *UK*. Yellow-
bodied pattern – shows that
Président Billard is the
same.
4 Baigent's Brown – *UK*.
Variant style, but with wings.
Very long springy hackles
sparsely applied with a shorter
hackle incorporated,

also sparsely.
5 Whirling Dun – *Australia/
Tasmania*. The original UK
pattern was a representation
of the autumn dun *Ecdyonurus
longicauda*, it is thought.
6 Sand Fly – *Germany*. If this
is No 11 of the patterns in
Ronalds' *The Fly-fisher's
Entomology*, it is interesting
to see how that sedge style has
taken the guise of an upwing,
although the tying ingredients
are much the same.
7 Gold-Ribbed Hare's Ear –
UK/general. Longstanding no-
hackle pattern. The hare's ear
fibres must be well picked out.
8 Greenwell's Glory (Dark)
– *New Zealand*. A variation
peculiar to New Zealand.
Body dark olive green floss.

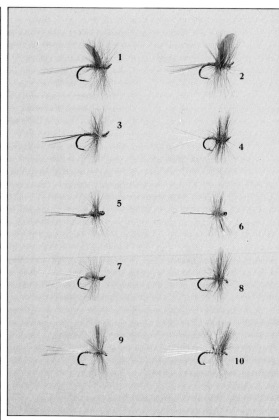

1 Orange Quill – *UK*. This is considered to be one of the best imitations of the blue-winged olive, particularly in late evening light. Wings optional.
2 Ginger Quill – *UK*. Used to imitate the paler olives and pale wateries. Wings optional.
3 Halford's Ginger Quill – *UK*. F.M. Halford, the "father" of classification of dry fly fishing, devised with care a large number of "exact imitations". This blue-winged olive imitation captures the brownish olive of the legs and the hazy blue of the insect's wings by using two hackles.
4 Blue-Winged Olive (BWO) – *UK*. Imitates one of the few medium-sized upwings

in the UK *(Ephemerella ignita)* with three tails.
5 Lunn's Particular – *UK*. Designed by William Lunn, keeper on the Test at Stockbridge. A 1917 pattern, possibly the first to use stripped hackle stalk as a body material.
6 Moucheron Spinner – *France*. View from above.
7 Tup's Indispensible – *UK*. A deservedly popular fly designed by R.S. Austin in 1900. Wool in body taken from specific part of male sheep.
8 D 7 – *Switzerland*.
9 Moucheron Ailes Gingembre – *France*.
10 Fibre des Hackles Gingembre – *France*.

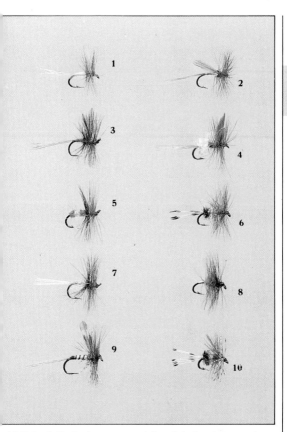

1 D 6 – *Switzerland*.
2 Exquisit Flying –
Germany.
3 Dark Olive – *Ireland*.
4 Beaverkill – *USA*. A
pattern gaining in popularity
in the UK as an olive
representation. The female is
given the egg sac; omit it for
males.
5 Caperer – *UK*. A sedge,
Halesus radiatus or *H.
digitatus*. Large and cinnamon
coloured. On the River Test
the name is also applied to
Sericostoma personatum, which
is Halford's Welshman's
button. Many of the
generalized sedge patterns are
used. Illustrated is Lunn's
dressing.
6 Panama – *France/Germany*.

One of the best known and
commonly fished of the
Continental patterns. Floats
well and looks well in all light
conditions.
7 Borchgrevink's Fancy –
Norway/Denmark/Sweden.
8 Tricolore – *Germany*. Very
similar to **Traun** pattern
borrowed from France.
9 FRZ Panama – *Germany*.
Borrowed from France;
variation apparent.
10 Superirresistible –
France.

1 Driffield Dun – *UK*.
Upwing imitation of
generalized nature evolved
round the Yorkshire
chalkstream, the Driffield
Beck.
2 Bulman's Favourite – *New
Zealand*.
3 Owaka – *Japan*. Like a very
dark **Orange Quill** – *UK*,
winged.
4 Dad's Favourite – *New
Zealand*. Evolved as a rejected
(on grounds of being too pale)
pattern tied as a Dark Red
Quill. It is therefore either a
Pale Dark Red Quill or a Dark
Ginger Quill!
5 Red Upright (Dark) – *New
Zealand*. Same as Red Quill
(NZ).
6 Arreflua – *Norway/*

Denmark/Sweden.
7 Golden Palmer – *Germany*.
General upwing or small
sedge-type pattern.
8 Wickham's Fancy – *UK/
general*. All-round proven
pattern – tied large and small,
wet and dry. General purpose.
Can represent upwings, sedges,
moths, etc.
9 Rio Grande Gold – *Japan/
USA*. Rio Grande King is the
"base" pattern. This is a
variation with gold tinsel body
instead of black chenille with
gold tip.
10 Hornsby Pheasant Tail –
UK. Variation on standard by
the addition of a dun shoulder
hackle. Used as alternative to
Sherry Spinner, **Red
Spinner**.

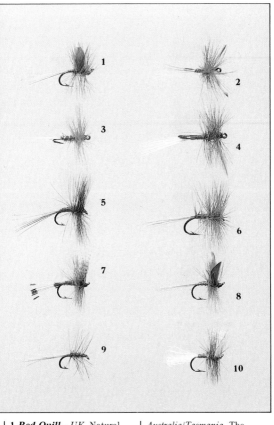

1 Red Quill – *UK*. Natural red hackle, quill body; a generalized pattern to represent many of the olives.
2 Lake Olive Spinner – *UK*. Natural: *Cloëon simile*, brownish olive as a dun. Viewed from above.
3 Red Spinner – *UK*. Term loosely applied to many spinners of upwings. More specifically it is applied to the female spinner of the olive dun. Alternative body tied with red silk.
4 Houghton Ruby (USD) – *UK*. Initially designed by W.J. Lunn, keeper of the Houghton Club on the River Test, to imitate the female spinner of the iron blue.
5 Red Spinner Hackle –

Australia/Tasmania. The turkey dun *(Atalophlebia costalis)* turns into the large red spinner.
6 Macquarie Red – *Australia/ Tasmania*. One of the Maury Wilson patterns.
7 Abbey Fly – *Norway/ Denmark/Sweden*. Accords with the US Abbey Fly.
8 Skittfiske – *Norway/ Denmark/Sweden*.
9 Europa Furnace – *France*. A very lightly dressed palmer-style fly. Riding high, it represents upwing duns or smaller sedges. Can represent emergers.
10 BWO Polywing – *Ireland*. Rather than quill wing or hackle point wing, this tying has "modern" material.

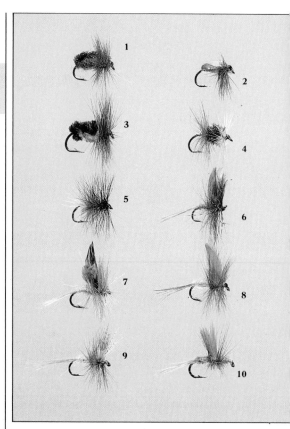

1 Green Beetle – *New Zealand*. There are two green beetles in New Zealand: *Pyronota festiva*, which is slightly smaller than the *Chlorochiton* species.
2 Manuka Beetle – *New Zealand*. Wing cases of green peacock herl are sometimes tied on these patterns.
3 Christmas Beetle – *Australia/Tasmania*.
4 Renegade – *USA*. An Idaho pattern of some antiquity. Colour order of hackle placement is a point of preference.
5 Tricolour – *USA*. Similar patterns suitably translated in Germany and France. Evidence of Bivisible style, but no tails.

6 March Brown (Male) – *UK*. Naturals: early season, *Rithrogena haarupi*; late season, *Ecdyonurus venosus*. UK tyings nearly all include partridge hackles and/or wings.
7 March Brown – *New Zealand*. Keith Draper suggests that this pattern can represent the *Deleatidium* group of upwings.
8 March Brown – *New Zealand*.
9 March Brown – *USA*. *Ephemera compar*, the western brown drake, has also the vernacular name of march brown. *Stenonema vicarium* carries the same name.
10 March Brown Thorax – *USA*.

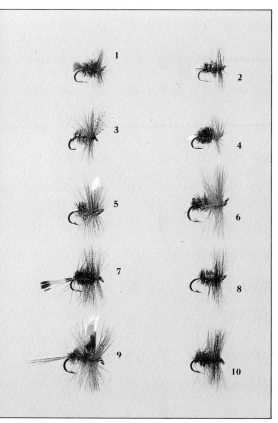

1 Red Tag – *UK/general*. A successful general purpose fly that has performed well at home and abroad for years. Outstanding for grayling, but trout take it well in a wide variety of sizes and styles.
2 Terry's Terror – *UK*. Another excellent Peter Deane pattern. Originated with Dr Cecil Terry on the Berkshire Kennet. General purpose fly. Rib is copper.
3 Pont Audemer Jaune – *France*.
4 Treacle Parkin – *UK*. Companion fly to **Red Tag**, but tied with yellow tag.
5 Coachman – *UK/general*. Long-lived standard, popular generally. Valuable at dusk because the white wings show

well. Wet or dry, lake or river, a good realiable pattern.
6 Hackle-point Coachman – *UK/general*. A variation. Wings may be also tied sloping, sedge-style in both hair-wing and standard quill wing.
7 Zwars Geni – *Africa*.
8 Coch-y-bondhu – *UK/general*. See Wet.
9 Peveril-of-the-Peak – *New Zealand*. General purpose fly. White tips to wings aid visibility at dusk or on dark water. Possibly a better dry fly than wet.
10 Double Hackle Cocky – *Australia/Tasmania*. Added palmer hackle to the standard pattern.

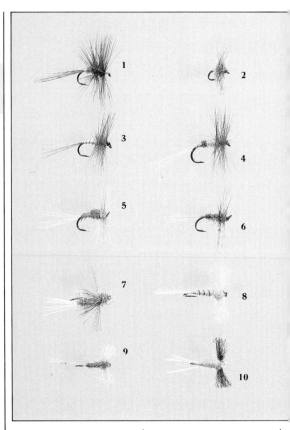

1 Orange Furnace –
Australia/Tasmania.
2 Traun Claire – *France*. In
the Bivisible style. Similar to
Tricolore.
3 Penstock Spinner –
Australia/Tasmania. Lacks the
brown hackle point wings of
the Penstock Brown.
4 George's Ghost –
Australia/Tasmania. A Maury
Wilson pattern.
5 Kite's Imperial – *UK*.
Named after Oliver Kite,
nymph fisher in the Sawyer
style. Pattern developed in
1962. Grey tails for early
season, honey-coloured for the
summer. Form thorax with
excess body material.
6 Claret Dun – *UK*. Natural:
Leptophlebia vespertina.

Unusual in that natural has
three tails. Some patterns use
dun rather than badger hackle.
7 Magic Spinner Buck –
Germany.
**8 Polywing Spinner Brown
Drake** – *USA*. Polywing is a
modern artificial fly-tying
material with translucency
and load-bearing capacity in
the surface film.
9 Rusty Polywing Spinner –
USA. More generalized – for
the spinners that have reddish
brown bodies. Used to
simulate the male spinner of
Ephemerella subvaria.
**10 Speckled Polywing
Spinner** – *USA*. Naturals:
Callibaetis coloradensis or *C.
nigritus*, primarily lake-
dwelling upwings.

1 Bogong Moth – *Australia/Tasmania*. These insects feed on honey in black ti-trees. When thirsty they head for water.

2 Allrounder – *UK*. John Ketley pattern. Also tied wet, when it can look either like a sedge struggling in the surface or a small minnow.

3 Hornberg – *USA*. Although initially a trout fly, has proved very effective for Atlantic salmon. Even when it eventually sinks, it continues to take fish under the surface.

4 Henryville Special – *USA*. Perhaps originated in Britain. Resurrected by Hiram Brobst to be named after stretch of Brodheads Creek. Body originally red, but improved by being tied green.

5 Sand Sedge – *France*. See **Sand Fly**.

6 Roman Moser Sedge – *Germany*. Traun River Products winging material which is woven cloth.

7 Mallard Sedge – *Ireland*. Rolled mallard breast feather wing.

8 Europa 12 – *Norway/Denmark/Sweden*.

9 Universelles – *Germany*. Very popular continental sedge-type pattern in a range from quite large to very small indeed. Probably would represent needle flies well.

10 Exquisit Rot – *Germany*. Also tied yellow. Thin wing resembles that of stoneflies of the needle fly/willow fly style.

1 Korksedge Natur –
Germany. Also yellow-bodied.
2 Cinnamon Sedge – *Italy*.
Wings are tied overlapping at
the body, separating at the
bend of the hook. Body
heavily palmer-hackled.
3 Marbled Sedge – *France*.
4 Brown Tent-wing Caddis
– *USA*. Note wing tied on
after hackle for this style.
5 FRZ Sedge – *Germany*.
Style borrowed from France.
Hackle-tip wings.
6 Altiere – *Germany*.
7 Oak Fly – *UK*. Terrestrial
(family *Leptidae*), also known
as down-looker, woodcock fly,
or cannon fly. See also **Mole
Fly**, which is also used to
imitate this insect. In evidence
in May and June. Small oak

fly in July and August.
8 Cinnamon Sedge – *UK*.
Natural insect: *Limnophilus
lunatus*. Body of male tends to
green, female to brown. A
good general fly. Takes
grayling as well as brown and
rainbow trout.
9 Murragh (Murrough) –
Ireland. Known as bustard in
parts of England. The natural
is *Phryganea grandis* or *P.
striata*, the large red sedge or
great red sedge. The natural is
sometimes used for dapping.
Activity starts at dusk, in
May, through to the end of the
season.
10 Hairwing Sedge –
Ireland.

1 Small Brown Fluttering Sedge – *USA*. Floating sedge patterns tied to embrace an "active" style of dry fly fishing, when the fly is given movement to disturb the water in a natural way, instead of producing "drag" This feature is also found in the **Richard Walker Sedge**.
2 Red Sedge – *UK*. See **Murragh**.
3 Highland Dun – *Australia/ Tasmania*. This tying is markedly sedgelike, but the natural, the large grey dun, or great lake dun (*Tasmanophlebia lacustris*) is an upwing.
4 Grannom – *UK*. The natural fly is *Brachycentrus subnubilis*, a diurnal sedge, sometimes called greentail

because the female carries a green egg sac. Illustration shows the browner end of the spectrum of imitations. Some are tied much more grey, and some have a more pronounced egg sac.
5 Richard Walker's (Red) Sedge – *UK*. Designed for "active" use. Tied with extra long throat hackles and water-shedding hackle-fibre wing.
6 Sedge Marron – *France*. Rolled bunched wing.
7 Great Red Sedge – *Ireland*. Variation on **Murragh**.
8 Gelbkorp Sedge – *Germany*. Single wing, varnished.
9 Traun Sedge – *Germany*. Similar winging to **Great Red Sedge**.

1 Hoolet – *UK*. Wing should
be tied from owl feather. This
possibly gives the pattern its
name because the owl is called
the hoolet in some areas. Moth
or sedge imitation.
2 Golden Stone – *USA*.
Similar to Sofa Pillow. Both
possible imitations of the adult
Acroneuria california,
emerging in early June on
many Oregon rivers.
3 Ragot Mai – *France*.
Mayfly imitation, as are most
of the following patterns.
Cream, grey, olive and green
mayflies to be seen in
appropriate sections. Ragot is
a most illustrious French
tackle company.
4 Cutwing ParaMay (Light)
– *Norway/Denmark/Sweden*.

Standard parachute style
hackle but borrowing from
USA's Harry Darbee for the
style of extended body. This
gives a good silhouette,
provides tail fibres and is
exceptionally lightweight.
5 Lunn's Spent Gnat – *UK*.
Illustrated from above,
showing extended wings of
adult.
6 Mai Parachute Brune –
France.
7 Vulgata – *France*. Name
taken from Latin classification
of insect it represents
(*Ephemera vulgata*). Fan-wing
style, which has lost favour in
the UK. *E. vulgata* is the
slightly less common of the
two mayflies, *E. danica* being
paler and greener.

1 Maifliege Braun –
Germany.
2 Korkmai Braun –
Germany. Cork bodies have a
long history. Their use has
been largely superseded by
better modern materials of
closed-cell foam.
3 Brown Mayfly – *USA.* In
America the word mayfly is
synonymous with upwing flies.
In the UK mayfly is specific:
Ephemera danica, E. vulgata
or, rarely, *E. lineata.* This
pattern could be chosen to
represent *Hexagenia recurvata.*
4 Bavaria Maifliege Spezial
– *Germany.*
5 Brown Drake – *USA.*
6 Straddlebug Mayfly –
Ireland. Classically this style is
fished in the surface film

rather than as a true floater.
Huge variety of dressings, but
style should contain very long
fibres (swept well back) of
partridge (English or French)
or waterfowl feathers.

123

1 Mallard Medicine – *UK*.
Slimline, tail-less version of
Teal Blue & Silver. Body
silver paint or silver Sellotape
rather than traditional tinsels.
**2 Hair-winged Teal Blue &
Silver** – *Wales/UK*. Grey
squirrel in place of teal for the
wing. Also with black floss silk
body, silver rib.
**3 Blue Black & Badger
Tandem** – *Wales/UK*. In the
Terror or Demon style. Hooks
may be doubles. Bodies may
be silver tinsel.
4 Blue Terror – *UK*. This is
a style adaptation, for a long
slender dressing but still light
enough to be easily fly cast.
5 Teal Medicine – *UK*.
Lighter version of **Mallard
Medicine**. Also dressed with

wigeon feather.
6 Falkus Sunk Lure – *UK*.
To be fished deep sunk. The
Demon and Terror patterns of
the early part of the century
have received new enthusiasm
in recent years.
**7 Mallard Wing Silver
Body** – *Wales/UK*. Darker
version of **Teal Blue &
Silver**. Black head. Contrast
with **Medicines** with red
heads and slimmer, unribbed
silver bodies.
**8 Black & Peacock Wing,
Silver Body** – *Wales/UK*.
Variation on preceding; dark;
silver and blue beneath.

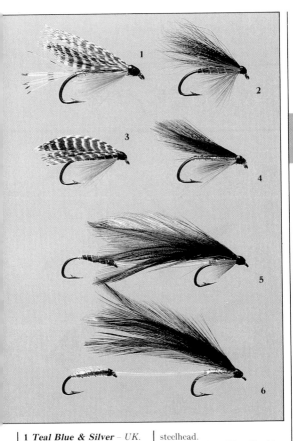

1 Teal Blue & Silver – *UK*.
Longstanding attractor/small
fish imitation. The barred teal
suggests the darker mottled
back of a bait fish, and the
blue hackle enhances the
silvery flash of the body. Also
known as Teal & Silver. It is
one of a series within the style
of traditional loch and sea-
trout flies with the teal wing.
**2 Black Wing, Black Body,
Silver Rib** – *Wales/UK*. Black
stoat's tail or other black hair
for the wing.
**3 Teal Wing, Black Body,
Silver Rib** – *Wales/UK*. A
darker (by virtue of black silk
body) version of **Teal Blue &
Silver**. Very similar to Salmon
Blue Charm, which is also
dressed for sea-trout and

steelhead.
**4 Black Wing, Blue Hackle,
Silver Body** – *Wales/UK*.
Black cock hackle points.
5 Black Tandem – *Wales/
UK*. Black cock hackle wing.
Alternative, black hair wing.
**6 Blue Black & Silver
Tandem** – *Wales/UK*.
Darkest illustrated of the
themes based loosely on **Teal
Blue & Silver**. Substitute
black hackle (or black hair if
so tied) with cuckoo or
Plymouth Rock hackles, and
another version of a **Teal
Blue & Silver** tandem. The
varieties on the illustrated
themes are endless, but the
Welsh, with important sea-
trout fisheries, consider all the
variations worthwhile.

125

1 Blackie – *Wales*.
Recommended as tail fly on a
quick-sinking line. Black
favoured for dark and cold
conditions. Tied also as single
fly, or with flying treble
(illustrated) or tandem. As
standard single, it shows
success as a reservoir trout
standard. "Secret weapon"
references relate to flying
trebles. Any of the sea-trout
patterns may be tied in this
style.
2 Badger Tandem – *Wales/
UK*.
3 Butcher – *UK*. Orginal is
the pattern shown, winged
either with crow feather or
iridescent blue duck wing
feather, silver body and black
hackle. The series developed

from it. Substitute the hackle
to accord with the name:
Canary Butcher (yellow),
Claret Butcher (dark claret),
and Kingfisher Butcher (blue
tail and wing with orange
hackle), **Bloody Butcher** (red
hackle), and Irish Butcher
(yellow palmered hackle added
to standard dressing).
4 Bloody Butcher – *UK*. To
show a variation within the
Butcher series.
5 Butcher Lure – *UK/
Kashmir*. Singles in range of
standard series used as well as
the tandem, in Kashmir, etc.
6 Kingsmill – *Ireland*.
Originally the pattern lacked
the topping over. Later
adaptation is inclusion of a
fluorescent green tag.

1 Blackbird – *USA*. Also a land-locked salmon pattern. There are many tyings similar to this i.e., black body, black wing, black hackle and jungle cock sides. Steelhead pattern.

2 Turkey Orange & Gold – *UK*. Great enrichment of colour over plain Turkey & Gold, which in Ireland may be known as Turkey Tip.

3 Turkey & Silver – *UK*. Very similar to **King Butcher** from Africa.

4 Bibio – *Ireland*. From the Sid Knight catalogue. Useful on the Irish loughs Corrib and Mask. Can be tied in four sections: black/red/black/red.

5 Black Prince – *USA*. Various body materials are popular variations. Pattern illustrated shows ⅕ floss silk, ⅘ black chenille. Other ties use yellow wool/black wool. Steelhead pattern.

6 Camasunary Killer – *Scotland*. Originated in Jedburgh, near the River Tweed. Correctly tied with extra long black hackle. Sea-trout pattern.

7 Skunk – *USA*. Variant styles. Wing may be tied before the hackle (illustrated) or laid over the hackle, as in the basic Standard Skunk. Steelhead pattern.

8 Alexandra – *UK*. A well-spoken of fly, but fish are not wholeheartedly attracted. Sea-trout/trout pattern. adopted as a standard steelhead pattern.

1 Watson's Fancy Lure –
UK/Kashmir. Tandem of *2*.
2 Watson's Fancy – *UK*.
Another old favourite for sea-
trout. The body is optionally
silk or seal's fur or wool. The
wing is black crow, mallard
speculum, or blackcock tail.
3 Black Zulu – *UK*. A
palmered-style fly, perhaps
representing hatching
chironomids, with an addition
of red for its tail as an
attraction. A reliable standby
among the traditional loch/
sea-trout flies. Also Blue Zulu.
4 Black Pennell – *UK*. The
original dressing by
Cholmondeley-Pennell had a
golden pheasant topping for
its tail. Modern dressings use
tippet. The body is either

black floss, black wool or
black seal's fur. The hackle
should be long. Sea-trout/trout
pattern.
5 Sooty Olive Mallard Wing
– *Ireland/UK*. Sooty olive is
the body colour, in seal's fur.
The wet fly has mallard wings;
the dry, cock blackbird wings.
Sea-trout/trout pattern.
6 Mallard & Gold – *UK*. One
of the Mallard series. In
smaller sizes for trout.
**7 Golden Olive Mallard
Wing** – *Ireland/UK*. Golden
pheasant tippet and crest tail
sometimes included.
8 Golden Olive Blae Wing –
Ireland. As with most of the
Irish patterns of this style,
tied for both trout and sea-
trout.

1 Boss – *USA*. Variation: where black – orange; where orange – black. Steelhead pattern.

2 Claret Pennell – *UK*. Tied with seal's fur. Alternatives are floss, silk or wool. Blue Pennell is quite similar to Donegal Blue, which has its moments as a bob fly for sea-trout, trout and salmon.

3 Dunkela – *UK*. Traditional loch/sea-trout pattern. Jungle cock sides not always included. Sometimes palmer-hackled with natural red hackle. Throat hackle of blue jay sometimes omitted. Dry pattern tied with grouse wings or mallard.

4 Mallard & Silver – *UK*.

5 Fiery Brown – *Ireland/UK*.

One of the oldest Irish patterns. More involved dressings have underwing of tippet strands, peacock sword and red ibis beneath the bronze mallard. Also Fiery Brown & Yellow, with posterior third of body golden olive wool or yellow floss. Fiery Brown & Blue, with dark blue hackle. Sea-trout/trout pattern.

6 Harry Tom – *Wales*. Popular on North Wales rivers such as the Ogwen. Used day and night. Often used in small sizes as a dropper above a large lure.

7 Cock Robin – *Ireland/UK*. Also known as Jointer or Jointed Mallard or Mallard & Mixed.

1 Towy Topper – *Wales*. The Towy is an outstanding sea-trout river. This is a pattern slightly out of the public eye but with a reputation in smaller sizes. Also tied dry.

2 Teifi Terror – *Wales*. The tying from a single has now more commonly become a tandem. Has a flashy attraction in peaty water, either fished deep on quick-sink lines or with lighter tackle.

3 Dyfi Bumble – *Wales*. This river has a grand sewin (sea-trout) reputation, and its fly, also tied in tandem, takes its share. Sometimes the body is lightly palmered.

4 Dai Ben – *Wales*. Very popular in the 1950s and

1960s. Used day and night. Good reputation on the River Towy.

5 Conway Red – *Wales*. An update on the Conway Badger, and bulkier. Tied without a hackle. Badger hair used for the wing, or its substitute is grey squirrel. Recommended as a floating-line fly.

6 Grey Monkey – *UK*. Trout pattern in smaller sizes. Larger for sea-trout, and in appropriate style for salmon. Green Monkey has fluorescent green tag.

7 Queen of the Waters – *USA*. Squirrel hair wing alternative.

8 Professor – *USA/Canada*. Traditional US trout as well as steelhead pattern.

1 Peacock Lure – *UK/Kashmir*. Tandem of traditional UK wet fly. Used as single also in small sizes.
2 Gold Invicta – *UK*. One of the **Invicta** variants. A trout pattern also.
3 Wickham's Fancy Lure – *UK/Kashmir*. Less likely as a dressing to be tied as a lure than the usual standard wet trout attractor patterns. Used in singles as well.
4 Grenadier – *UK*. Recent considerable popularity tied in Competition rules sizes and fished loch-style. Developed in the Chew and Blagdon reservoirs at the turn of the century. Tied bushy as bob fly (illustrated in this style).
5 Soldier Palmer – *UK*. Tied here bob fly style, with addition of red tag. Sedge/beetle representation. Tied small for trout.
6 Greenwell's Glory (Hackled) – *Scotland*. A heavy dressing as a bob fly. As such, by its action, it becomes a general pattern of moth, sedge, emerger appearance.
7 Rasputin – *UK*. Started as a reservoir lure. Surface wake fly also used for sea-trout. Because it is made from closed-cell foam, it is buoyant and can therefore be fished on quick-sink line at great depth without fouling river bed or lake bed. Considerable bulk.

1 Peter Ross Lure – *UK*.
Tandems or Terrors have a
long history. Mostly in Britain
they have been designed and
used for sea-trout, so standard
sea-trout patterns have been
adapted to this style.

2 Peter Ross – *Scotland*. One
of the best known and most
widely used of the traditional
loch/sea-trout flies. The half
silver and half red body is a
great improvement on the all
red-bodied Teal & Red.

3 Silver Hilton – *USA*.
Steelhead pattern. Also Gold
Hilton.

4 Worm Fly – *UK*. Early
recommendations were for it
to be fished deep and slow
after dark. Nowadays it seems
to be in wider use, particularly

in large reservoirs. Similar is
Dambuster.

5 Teal & Green – *UK*. Quite
a few variations exist. The
illustration is a good standard
but alternatives include black
throat hackle, teal fibres for
the tail, light green palmered
hackle, with blue jay throat
hackle, and wings underlaid
with blue peacock.

6 Teal & Green Lure – *UK/
Kashmir*. Tandem of standard
for trout and sea-trout.

7 Jungle Lure – *UK/
Kashmir*. Tandem tying of UK
standard pattern. Also used in
singles.

8 Haslam – *Wales*.
Variations: Andalusian or
white body hackles; false blue
jay hackle and orange tag.

1 *Invicta Bob Fly* – *UK*.
Contrast the dressing with
Invicta. Extra thick hackling,
body and throat, to force the
fly to the top and create
surface disturbance.
2 *Invicta* – *UK*. This is the
standard. Other Invicta
patterns proliferate. The
standard is considered a good
imitation of adult and pupal
sedge flies.
3 *Silver March Brown Lure*
– *UK/Kashmir*. Tandem of
standard variation of a trout
and sea-trout pattern. Used
also as single, and other
dressings of March Brown also
used.
4 *Silver March Brown* –
UK.
5 *Mallard & Claret Lure* –

UK/Kashmir. An old standby
in so many waters as a single;
adapted as a tandem. Singles
also used in Kashmir.
6 *Grouse & Claret* – *UK*.
Wide-ranging series including:
Grouse & Black (can have
underwing of tippet); Grouse
& Blue; Grouse & Green (can
have underwing); Grouse &
Gold and Grouse & Jay (blue
jay hackle).
7 *Mallard & Claret* – *UK*. A
traditional loch and sea-trout
fly that in Ireland has
remained in favour. In
England it is finding favour
again on big reservoirs after
two decades out of esteem.
8 *Woodcock & Red* – *UK*.
Traditional loch-style trout fly
in small sizes.

1 Gray Ghost – *USA/Canada*. This is distinct from the New Zealand **Grey Ghost**. It is one of the better known transatlantic streamers seeing some increasing trout use in the UK. It is an exceptional pattern for landlocked salmon. It carries a suggestion of the foodfish smelt of freshwaters. **Lady Ghost** resembles it in some ways. **Black Ghost** involves less complex tying. All these streamers may be tied in large sizes and tandems.

2 Silver Tandem – *Wales/ UK*. This style of Mylar tubing over the link is found also in saltwater patterns such as the Sandeel.

3 Gold Tandem – *Wales/UK*. Mylar is used for the body material, enveloping the link between the hooks.

4 Bloody Butcher – *USA*. This is sufficiently different from the Picket Pin to warrant individual designation. It is favoured during the stonefly hatch. It is used also for steelhead. Distinct from the UK trout/ sea-trout pattern of the same name.

1 *Thor* – *USA*. This is a
standard steelhead pattern. It
is found on most
"recommended" lists.

2 *Skykomish Sunrise* –
USA. Strong fish with strong
teeth need strong flies. This
pattern emphasizes the stout
wire hook, thick, water-
absorbent dressing, and dense
hackle and wing. The pattern
is sometimes given a flat silver
tinsel tip.

3 *Chief Needabeh* – *USA*.
Named after an Indian Chief,
it is similar to Preston
Jennings' Lord Iris pattern. A
variation with fluorescence
included is called The Chief. It
is also similar to ***Whisky Fly***,
Dunkeld, Ravenglass, Orange
Bucktail, and Orange

Streamer. It is used for
landlocked salmon, char,
trout, and steelhead. It can be
dressed up to 4¼ inches long.

4 *Comet* – *USA*. This is a
steelhead pattern, which is
also found with bead eyes. The
throat hackle may include a
yellow under-hackle. There is
also Silver Comet, Gold
Comet, etc. Fluorescent
materials form a variation. It
is recommended by Lefty
Kreh for Pacific salmon, or
flies of similar style.

1 Little Rainbow Trout –
USA/Canada. Also a trout
pattern.
2 Little Brown Trout –
USA/Canada. Also a trout
pattern.
3 Little Brook Trout – *USA/
Canada*. Also a trout pattern.
4 Dark Edson Tiger – *USA/
Canada*. Also for trout and
landlocked salmon. Tied up to
4½ inches, also as tandem. Tied
in miniature for the
illustration.
5 Anson – *USA/Canada*. Also
for trout and landlocked
salmon. Tied in miniature for
the illustration – can be up to
4½ inches.
6 Light Edson Tiger – *USA/
Canada*. Also for trout and
landlocked salmon. Tied in

miniature for the illustration.
Can be up to 4½ inches, and
also tied as a tandem.
7 Frances – *USA/Canada*.
Also trout and landlocked
salmon pattern. Tied in
miniature for the illustration.
Can be up to 4½ inches long,
and in tandem style.
8 Black Ghost – *USA/
Canada*. Not as complex as the
Gray Ghost. A simple black
body with white wing
streamer is mostly used. It is
tied up to 4 inches long,
sometimes in tandem. For
landlocked salmon, steelhead
and trout.

These streamers, and others
illustrated elsewhere, can have
considerable success with
Atlantic salmon.

1 Coachman Lure – *UK/
Kashmir*. Traditional popular
pattern in tandem style for
Indian fishing. Also used as a
single.
2 White Glo-bug – *USA*.
Steelhead egg pattern. *See also
Red Glo-bug*.
3 Whit's Double Egg Sperm
(Orange) – *USA*. Compare
with Pink. This has a marabou
wing and no central hackle.
4 Babine Special – *USA*.
Variation: extra intermediate
hackle red, with throat hackle
white; no wing. Some tyings
pronounce the double egg
effect by bulking up the
chenille body segments. It was
originally used on the Babine
River.

5 Whit's Double Egg Sperm
(Pink) – *USA*. **Double Flame
Egg** is similar.
6 Polar Shrimp – *USA*.
Steelhead pattern. Probably
started with polar bear hair
wing. Now white bucktail.
Variations are (1) body and
tail may be red; (2) body half
gold and half orange chenille;
(3) body fluorescent red or
fluorescent pink, with white
bucktail tied in at the head
and tail.
7 Red-Glo Bug – *USA*.
8 Single Egg – *USA*. From
the Orvis Tying Catalogue.
Glo-Bug yarn is applied like
Muddler-head deer hair, and
trimmed. Egg patterns
primarily for steelhead,
although also listed in Italy.

137

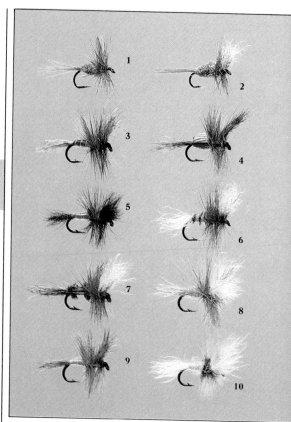

1 Rat-faced McDougal –
USA. Clipped deer hair body.
Possibly a forerunner in the
development of the
Irresistible. 1939 offspring of
the Beaverkill Bastard.
2 Irresistible – *USA*.
Credited to Harry Darbee as a
style. Stout body with
distinctive profile, and natural
buoyancy from the clipped
deer hair. Also White
Irresistible.
3 Red Wulff – *USA*. Lee
Wulff's patterns were devised
in the 1930s and have become
standards all over the world.
4 Goofus Bug – *USA*.
Originally known as Horner's
Deer Hair, the body, tail and
wings are of deer hair. Red
and Yellow are standards.

5 Black Wulff – *USA*. Also
seen with black body. Suitable
for trout, steelhead and
salmon.
6 Wasp Wulff – *USA*.
7 Royal Wulff – *USA*.
Following the immense
popularity of the **Royal
Coachman**, a Wulff-style
pattern of **Royal Coachman**
was inevitable.
8 Grizzly Wulff – *USA*.
9 Ausable Wulff – *USA*. The
high-riding, robust dry flies
don't contain wolf hair, but
bucktail.
10 White Wulff – *USA*. A
noted taker of Atlantic
salmon. Tied up to 4 times the
illustrated size, it can attract
fish to rise, leading to their
taking a smaller pattern.

1 Loch Ordie Dapping –
UK. Originated from E R
Hewitt's Nevasink Spiders
used when he took summer
fishing from the Duke of
Atholl on Loch Ordie.
Subsequent patterns
incorporate flying trebles to
help hooking, although overall
weight is increased. For trout
as well as sea-trout.

2 Furnace Dapping – *UK.*
Dapping involves the use of a
long rod, and a line light
enough to be held out by the
wind, so that the fly alone is
on the water. No casting is
involved. The fly is induced to
dance on the surface, bobbing
along on the waves. All
dapping patterns are designed
for buoyancy. Any favourite

patterns may be appropriately
tied for dapping, and in a
variety of colour combinations
for easy visibility for the
fisherman.

3 Black Pennell Dapping –
UK. Extra bulk for dapping in
a renowned trout and sea-
trout pattern. Possible salmon
dry fly pattern.

4 Coch-y-bondhu Dapping
– *Wales.* An adaptation of the
standard famous dressing for
dappng.

5 Bivisible – *USA.*

6 Badger & Red – *USA.*

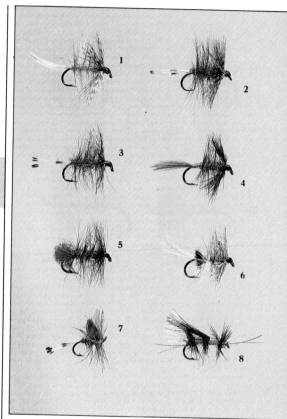

1 Golden Olive Bumble –
Ireland. Most highly
recommended of the Kingsmill
Moore Bumble series, where
buoyancy and sparkle are part
of the attraction. Colour
combination inspired by
Invicta.
2 Magenta Bumble –
Ireland.
3 Claret Bumble – *Ireland*.
Subtle blend of cock hackle
with fibre hackle suggests
movement. Incorporates
translucent effect with typical
subtle Irish colour blending.
4 Fiery Brown Bumble –
Ireland. Traditional Irish
colour is fiery brown. It is
entirely logical for this to be
included in this Bumble series
of sea-trout lough flies.

5 The Bruiser – *Ireland*.
Another of the Kingsmill
Moore Bumble series. Good for
brown trout and sea-trout on
dark days with low cloud and
showers.
6 Grey Ghost Bumble –
Ireland. Recommended by its
designer for days of diffused
light when underwater
visibility seems much
accentuated, and on very
bright days.
7 Hardy's Favourite – *UK/
general*. Tied wet and dry.
Originally trout and sea-trout
pattern; adopted for steelhead;
and highly favoured in New
Zealand.
8 Bird's Stone Fly – *USA/
NDS*. Originated by Calvin
Bird. Wings flattened.

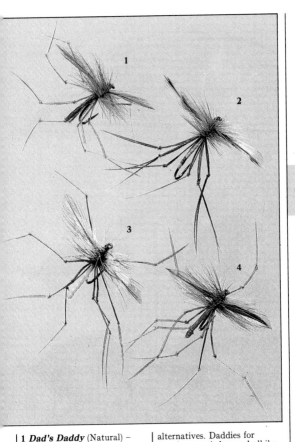

1 Dad's Daddy (Natural) – *General*. The crane fly is known as a Daddy or Daddy-long-legs, or Harry or Harry-long-legs. One of the Tipulidae, it lies inert, struggles, then lies inert again. "Natural" refers to the body colour. The various species that fall on the water range from greyish to orange, and dressings reflect this in body colour, hackle colour and wing colour.

2 Daddy-long-legs (Raffia) – *UK*. Bleached dried grass (raffia) is easily handled and just the colour for the bodies of some crane flies. Although traditional, it is not outmoded. The tying shown is on a long shank hook. Detached bodies are alternatives. Daddies for dapping are tied more bulkily than the dry fly pattern. Sometimes the effect of two on a single hook is made with four wings and two bodies.

3 Dad's Daddy (Green Fluorescent) – *General*. Legs are strands of cock pheasant tail feather with knotted joints. Alternative is knotted fine nylon.

4 Dad's Daddy (Red Fluorescent) – *General*. The red body colour is an extra attraction to a good imitative profile.

N.B. Daddies fished dry or dapped take brown trout as well as sea-trout, and may take salmon.

1 Black Power – *Norway*.
Big flies, big fish. Rather
stronger cold water needs large
flies. Modern components
incorporating marabou (eagle
was used for a few salmon
standards a long time ago).
Spey-type mobile palmer-
hackling and flashabou for
ribbing and throat hackle. As
yet there is no broad base of
experience in the UK for a
style as modern as this,
although flash strands are said
to enhance the usual tyings.
2 Black Dose – *UK/general*.
At one stage body was ⅓ light
blue seal's fur, ⅔ black seal's
fur; wing, two tippets back to
back, mixed wing over. No
jungle cock. Times change.
The simplified version is very

similar to the **Black Spean**.
3 Black Dose – *UK/general*.
Simplified West Country
version.
4 Black Doctor – *UK/general*.
This is the standard, easily
recognized by the red butt.
Often head varnish is also red.
Jungle cock omitted in early
tyings. Very similar: archaic
Sir Richard.
5 Black Doctor – *UK/general*.
Early patterns contained a
claret palmer hackle. The
mixed wing has been
dispensed with in this
simplified tying. One of a well
known quartet; **Black, Blue,
Silver** and **Helmsdale
Doctors**.

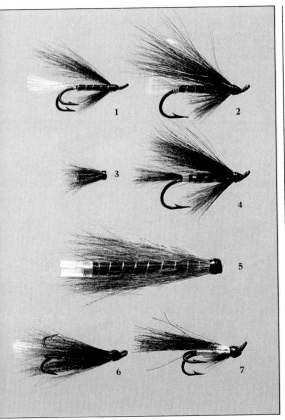

1 Stoat's Tail (Double) – *UK*. Standard style. A practical point about doubles is that they weigh more, and in most instances fish a little deeper. They also produce a more blocky silhouette.

2 Stoat Flash – *UK*. More pronounced yellow tail than standard, and inclusion of "flash" material in wing. Originally fibres from stoat's tail; now any fine black mobile hair.

3 Stoat's Tail (Tube) – *UK*. The sort of low-water summer fishing size. Plastic tube.

4 Black Bear/Green Butt – *USA/Iceland*. Variation on the standard pattern which has no distinctive butt. Also for Iceland, Black Bear/Red Butt.

5 Stoat's Tail (Tube) – *UK*. Another winging fibre that is large enough has to be found because the size has increased. True stoat's tail fibres are rarely long enough for the larger patterns.

6 Silver Stoat (Long-shank treble) – *UK*. Long-shank trebles have plenty of admirers. Silver body a variation on the standard. There are also red-bodied variants.

7 Black Sheep – *Iceland*. Very much exaggerated. With a longer wing is similar to the Collie Dog.

1 *Jeannie* (Double) –
Scotland/UK. One of the
summer-style patterns
developed on the
Aberdeenshire Dee; also
Jimmie, Jockie and *Logie*. In
the UK, at least, salmon
doubles come in three weights:
extra light wire, light wire and
standard.
2 *Jeannie* (hairwing – single)
– *Scotland/general*. Singles look
less stocky than doubles.
Which is more effective as a
hooking medium is debatable.
3 *Black Spean* – *Finland*.
Scottish pattern named after
northern West Coast river. If
body is tied $\frac{1}{3}$ yellow floss, $\frac{2}{3}$
black floss, becomes *Jeannie*.
4 *Black Body "A"* – *Finland*.
Notable exclusion of body or

throat hackle. Very simple.
5 *Black Fairy* – *Finland*.
There are also Irish tyings of
the same name: both with
bronze mallard wing, one with
jay throat, the other with
black palmer hackle over wool
body.
6 *Black Francis* – *Iceland*.
Bead eyes where whiskers join
the body. Also *Red Francis*
and Green Francis.
7 *Elver Fly* – *UK*. Designed
by Arthur Ransome of *Rod
and Line*. Traditional wing
feather is vulturine guinea
fowl. Tied also for seatrout.
8 *Sweep* – *UK*. Standard,
probably more popular outside
than inside UK. Illustrated
with gut-loop eye. Gut eyes
perish and may break.

1 **Namsen** – *Norway*. Named for a truly large river holding huge salmon. Distinguish this pattern from Kelson's Namsen – red, blue and claret seal's fur body, palmer-hackled with golden pheasant breast feather and tail fibre wing.

2 **Odd's Laksflua** – *Norway*. This pattern is also tied for trout and sea-trout. Wet and dry.

3 **Night Hawk** – *USA/ Canada*. Listed by Jorgensen and Wulff. An Ira Gruber pattern, for the Miramichi, initially.

4 **Black Body "B"** – *Finland*. Local adaptation of originally British fully dressed salmon style.

5 **Peter Paho** – *Finland*.

Fully dressed style showing traditional British influence.

6 **Finland No 3** – *Finland*.

7 **Akroyd** – *Scotland*. One of the most famous of the Dee-style strip-wing standard salmon flies. Cinnamon turkey alternative to white swan wing. Golden pheasant topping a brilliant substitute for yellow hackle on posterior half of body. Style must be slender and attenuated. Jungle cock angled downwards, as in other Dee-style patterns.

8 **Green Butt Spey** – *Sweden*. Derivation of spey style from Scotland and American/ Canadian dressing. Tied in large sizes to 9/o singles, 5/o doubles.

1 Blue Charm – *UK/general.*
One of the best known small
summer patterns.
Theoretically, blue flies appear
more attractive in the blue .
light of the early morning, and
silver tinsel backing the blue
hackle enhances this.

2 Blue Charm (Double) –
UK/general. Traditional
summer pattern on River Dee,
now general. Crossed the
Atlantic very successfully.
Jorgensen's tying varies by
including underwing of pine
squirrel tail and dark (not
bright) blue hackle.

3 Blue Charm – *UK.* West
Country version.

4 Hairy Mary – *General.* As
soon as the ease of tying and
the satisfactory result of hair-
wing flies was noted, patterns
evolved in parallel with the
existing feather-wing tyings.

5 Hairy Mary (Waddington)
– *UK/general.* Waddingtons
are usually tied in larger sizes.
Small Waddingtons tend to be
rather stocky.

6 Thornton (Tube) – *UK/
general.* Example of a small
dressing. Easier with hair than
with feather materials. Result
is probably just a silhouette to
the fish's eye, all the same.

7 Hairy Mary (Tube) – *UK/
general.* Large example shown.
Compare it for size with the
Thornton, which is dressed
for low water, summer,
greased line/floating line
fishing, possibly for the same
size of salmon.

1 Silver Doctor – *UK/ general*. Doctors usually tied with red butt and red head. Series is **Black**, **Blue**, **Silver** and **Helmsdale Doctors**, wing components nowadays remaining much the same in each designation. Large quantity of trout, sea-trout, and steelhead patterns of this name, being basically simplifications.

2 Silver Doctor – *UK*. West Country version.

3 Silver Wilkinson (Hair) – *UK*. This pattern has been dressed extra long and mobile in style. It is a modern hair adaptation of a gaudy pattern classed originally as a Tweed fly – a complex traditional whole feather/built wing standard.

4 White Doctor (Low-water) – *Ireland/general*. Example of a low-water dressing. Light wire hook, and very spare in material. Made a name for itself with sea-trout in the West Country.

5 Silver Wilkinson – *UK/ general*. This is about as large as single-hook or double-hook dressings are tied nowadays in the UK. The better hooking of large waddingtons and tubes is chosen.

6 Silver Wilkinson (Tube) – *UK/general*. Tied in its simplest form. Jungle cock sides are a reasonable option.

1 White Wing (Tube) – *Scotland*. For long a feather-tied Tweed fly, with a new lease of life as a hair wing pattern. Probably the biggest sales at Melrose on the Tweed at the end of the season are the White Wing and the Comet.

2 Blue Doctor – *Scotland/general*. Jungle cock not included in the earlier tyings.

3 Gordon – *UK*. Old standard but even in 1900 causing much discussion among leading authorities about its components. The largest sizes incorporated golden pheasant sword feathers as an underwing.

4 Blue Doctor – *Scotland/general*. Muted West Country version of the standard.

5 Blue Highlander – *Scotland/general*. Variation of the old standard, the **Green Highlander**.

6 White/blue/red body (Waddington) – *General*. Some authorities do not place too much importance on pattern or colour for the largest deep-sunk flies – depth and speed being more important. Many of the patterns are described rather than named.

1 Green Butt – *USA/Iceland.*
Very similar to Black Bear/
Green Butt but has throat of
black hackle and additional
blue hair in the wing.
2 Red Butt – *USA/Iceland.*
3 Aron of Neiden – *Norway.*
See also **Silver Doctor, Teal
Blue & Silver**.
4 Le Ny Paon – *France.*
Peacock sword fibres are quite
popular in a number of French
patterns. Other preferences are
wool or seal's fur bodies,
modest amounts of tinsel;
grey, cuckoo, or chinchilla
hackles.
5 Green Highlander –
Scotland/general. Many
accepted variations of a
standard tying; some insist on
whole feather tippet

underwing. Some prefer body
to include yellow seal's fur.
Francis Francis attributed it
to the Ness, with a strong
recommendation for its use on
the Carron.
6 Green Highlander – *UK/
general.* Mixed wing enveloped
by broad bronze mallard for
the West Country variation.
7 Wrack – *General.* Listed in
modern update of probably
the best of all salmon fly-tying
books, *How to Dress Salmon
Flies* by T.E. Pryce-Tannatt.
8 Turquoise – *France.* Simple
pattern; use of local game-bird
plumage. Here cock pheasant
tail fibre wing.

1 Jungle Master – *Sweden*. It has similarities to some shrimp patterns but is *much* larger.

2 Mar Lodge Variant – *Finland*. The original pattern includes jungle cock in the tail and has silver not gold tinsel. This is a Dee pattern but not Dee-style. The name is derived from a royal hunting lodge in Aberdeenshire near the River Dee.

3 Mar Lodge – *UK*. This is a West Country variation.

4 Lady Amherst – *UK/ general*. This is a pattern adopted by Poul Jorgensen, who in America has espoused the welfare of fully dressed traditional salmon flies. It is included in Lee Wulff's list.

5 Silver Grey – *UK*. This is a West Country version. The principle and style of the full tying remain similar, but the result is more muted and more simply dressed.

6 Gray's Silver Invicta – *UK*. This is a summer pattern, dressed long, thin and translucent on a light wire hook. It is a standard trout pattern adapted for salmon.

7 Silver Rat – *USA/Canada*. This is one of the Rat series, of which there are nine regular patterns. It was devised in 1911. Other Rats are illustrated on pages 151 and 152.

1 **Gray Rat** – *USA*.
2 **Finland No 5** – *Finland*.
This is made from modern
materials, rather than
following the traditional style.
Possible Rat influence.
3 **Silver, Pink and Black** –
Finland. Tied in low water
miniatures it closely resembles
summer salmon flies tied for
the Scottish Earn, a tributary
of the Tay.
4 **Black Rat** – *USA*.
5 **North Fork Spey** – *Sweden*.
This is a derivation of the
Scottish Spey style and an
American/Canadian pattern. It
is tied to the largest sizes for
strong Scandinavian rivers.
6 **Finland No 2** – *Finland*.
This resembles the 'upright'

styling of the Spey-style **Lady
Caroline**.
7 **March Brown** – *Finland*.
Just occasionally salmon flies
bear a resemblance to natural
insects. Salmon have been
observed to rise to the natural
march browns, and so a
variety of patterns have been
evolved which look natural.
8 **Le Ny Grise** – *France*. A
pattern from François Le Ny,
"perhaps the most noteworthy
salmon fisherman who has
ever fished the salmon rivers
of Brittany". Local traditions
recommend seal's fur or pig's
wool, supple hackling and
relatively sombre colouring.
Darker patterns of flies as the
season progresses.

1 Rusty Rat – *USA.* Hair-wing, thus "modern". The Rat series is named from the initials of *Roy Angus Thomson. See also Black Rat, Blue Rat, Gold Rat, Silver Rat, Gray Rat.*

2 Black Cosseboom – *USA/ general.* Jungle cock sides optional. Series includes Cosseboom (also called Cosseboom Special) with green body and tail, Gold, Orange, Peacock and Red Cossebooms. Successful patterns in Iceland and Scandinavia.

3 Silver Cosseboom – *USA/ general.* Jungle cock sides or optional. The Cossebooms originated as streamers on the Margaree River.

4 Garry (Feather-wing) – *UK/ general.* Shows how the feather dressed pattern differs from the derivative hair-winged.

5 Garry (Hair-wing) – *UK/ general.* Not always black palmer hackled. Singles, doubles, long-shank trebles, Waddingtons and tubes. With addition, to choice, in all styles of "flash" tinsel in the wing.

6 Bonny Charles – *UK.* Note woollen butt, instead of more usual herl.

7 Lemon Grey – *Ireland/ general.* Often given heavy bronze mallard overwing. Traditionally salmon fly heads were dubbed wool or herl. Now usually varnished black – red in the case of the Doctors.

1 Yellow Dog – *UK*. Very similar to USA's **Mickey Finn**. The tube extension, which shows translucent, allows the eye of the treble to be pulled up in line with the fly.

2 Waddington (Orange/Black with silver body) – *UK*. Waddingtons are articulated where the eye of the treble joins the shank of the fly. Tubes and Waddingtons are an improvement on very large singles or doubles, because they do not offer the same leverage.

3 Allan's Fancy (Tube) – *UK*. Three sets of winging/hackle, giving plenty of bulk. The heaviest tubes are brass, the medium ones aluminium, and the lightest are plastic. Very similar to Comet and Tadpole.

4 Waddington (Red/black/black & silver body) – *UK*. Now that traditional patterns have become outmoded in many instances, there are no effective names except for descriptions of modern hairwing dressings.

5 Dunkeld (Tube) – *UK*. This is a mixture of hair and feather. The emphasis in this illustration is on the shoulder hackle.

1 *No 1 Spey* – *Sweden*. Classic
derivative from the traditional
mobile style of the original
Spey patterns. Tied on singles
to 9/0 and doubles to 5/0.
Tubes are also tied
asymmetrically for Sweden,
with immensely long wing.
2 *Joe Brady* – *Finland*.
Yellow butt is an unusual
feature. Underwing (hidden) of
cinnamon turkey. In Pryce-
Tannatt the overwing is
omitted. His original dressing
included Indian crow cheeks;
today, substitutes must be
used. Perruche in 1922
included the Joe Brady in his
list of salmon patterns for
France in *La pêche de la truite
et du saumon à la mouche
artificielle*.

3 *No 2 Spey* – *Sweden*.
Derivation of standard
Scottish Spey patterns. Large
rivers mean large fish, hence
large flies. Tied in singles to
9/0, in doubles to 5/0. Collie
Dogs are tied much in the
style of 1 and 3.

1 Logie – *Scotland/general*.
Summer pattern from
Aberdeenshire Dee. Usually
tied low-water style, with
entire dressing shorter than
the hook shank.
2 Logie (Hair-wing) –
Scotland/general.
3 Lanctot – *Canada*. Complex
underwing veiled by yellow
Swan: red, blue swan, grey
mallard and grouse.
4 Helmsdale Doctor – *UK*.
Named after River Helmsdale
in northern Scotland. Pattern
one of a series of Doctors, but
didn't share quite the same
winging components.
5 Ballater – *UK*. Traditional-
style pattern. Name taken
from town on river Dee.
Another pattern from the

updated Pryce-Tannatt.
6 Lemon Wood Duck –
Finland. Fully dressed
traditional style. Close to the
Kelson Summer Duck pattern
which, in his time (1895), had
a killing reputation in large
sizes on the Sundal.
7 Dusty Miller Variant –
Finland. Variation consists of
deletion of golden olive body
hackle and dyed swan
elements of the wing. Hence
original British pattern is
more highly coloured. Variant
also substitutes gold rib for
original silver rib.
8 Dusty Miller – *UK*. West
Country version. Distinguished
from other silver-bodied
patterns by its embossed
tinsel.

1 Thunder & Lightning –
UK. One of the well known
standards. A first-choice fly on
many rivers. Hackles range
from fiery browns to reddish
orange.
2 Thunder & Lightning –
UK. West Country version.
3 Star of Lapland – *Norway/
Denmark/Sweden*. Use of Lady
Amherst pheasant tail feather
in conjunction with the hair
wing.
4 Golden Olive – *Ireland/
general*. Body may be golden
olive seal's fur throughout, or
graduate from golden olive at
tail to brown olive at head.
5 Silver-black – *Norway/
Denmark/Sweden*. Lady
Amherst wing.
6 Halpin – *Ireland*. Has

become a generalized pattern
for trout and salmon, although
designed for salmon. Said to
be good in peaty conditions.
7 Teno Star – *Finland*.
Difference of style in tail
dressing from standard
traditional flies for salmon.
Teno is the name of a river
called Tana by Norwegians.
8 Dunkeld – *UK*. Enlarged
dressing of a trout pattern of
the same name. In some
tyings there is an underwing
of golden pheasant tippet
beneath the bronze mallard,
and cheeks of blue kingfisher.
The silk tag is either orange or
sometimes gold floss silk. See
exaggerated aspect of one part
of this tying formula on page
155.

1 Thunder & Lightning
(Variant) – *Finland*. Variation
from standard British pattern
lies in broad red horns and
undyed gallina throat hackle.
2 Orange Blossom –
Norway. Also within the US
repertoire. Tied long-shank
treble by Jorgensen.
Originated with Mrs Carmelle
Bigaouette on the Matapedia.
3 Flash Black & Orange –
UK/general. In popular
combination of black and
orange, with or without silver
ribbing. Flash material and
more pronounced tail.
4 Black & Orange – *Wales*.
Quite a different effect from
the **Flash Black & Orange**
in this Welsh pattern, with an
orange throat hackle.

5 Munro Killer (Treble) –
UK. A modern variation of
the traditional **Thunder &
Lightning**. Originally tied with
black plastic body material.
**6 Low-water Yellow &
Black** – *UK*. Longshank
summer dressing. Style
variation with possibly better
hooking potential and better
entry than standard dressing
small salmon flies.
7 Yellow Torrish – *UK*.
Flies now known by this name
are modern simplifications of
an old feather-wing pattern –
see page 160.
8 Torrish (Tube) – *UK/
general*. The name is the same
but variation from the **Yellow
Torrish** is marked. Contrast
with **Torrish**, page 160.

1 *Shrimp* (Waddington) –
UK. Even though the colour
scheme remains similar to the
single-hooked version, the *style*
has altered, losing the fibrous
bulk at the tail.
2 *Lady Caroline* – *Scotland*.
This is a spey-style pattern:
relatively short bronze mallard
wings set "inverted boat-
shaped", and long heron or
spey cock hackles. In this
style also are Gold Riach,
Purple King, Green King,
Black King, Carron Fly,
Dallas Fly (winged with
cinnamon turkey), Glen Grant,
etc. The Lady Caroline in
various styles is probably the
only spey fly-style to remain
in modern use in the UK.
3 *Red Francis* – *Iceland*. This

is a Peter Deane tying. Also
Black Francis and Green
Francis (brownish-green
body).
4 *Prawn* (Tube) – *UK*. The
complexity of the double-hook
dressing is possible on a tube
or Waddington. Probably
superior hooking to singles or
doubles as soon as fly sizes
exceed $1\frac{1}{2}$ inches.

1 Shrimp (Salmon) – *UK*.
There are many variations on
the Shrimp theme. It is
assumed that forms of shrimp
constitute part of the deep-sea
feeding of the salmon, and
therefore they will welcome
this reminder when returned
to fresh water.

2 Stewart's Shrimp – *UK*. A
pattern with a red/black silk
body and golden pheasant
breast feather throat hackle
tied in over a dyed-red
squirrel hair wing.

3 Shrimp (Treble) – *UK*. Tied
with or without jungle cock,
to taste. Double or longshank
treble uses the shrimp-style
dressing probably better than
other hook styles, giving an
excellent silhouette.

4 Shrimp (Tube) – *UK*.
Colour but not shape remains
true to Shrimp patterns.

5 Krabla – *USA/Iceland*.
Prawn/shrimp imitation seen
from above. This is the
standard colour. Also Green
Krabla, and Yellow & Black
Krabla (yellow antennae and
rear half body, black tail and
front half body, with yellow
head).

6 Prawn Fly – *UK*. A
number of prawn patterns are
tied, most representing the
boiled rather than the natural
colour. The bulk and profile of
doubles and longshank trebles
suits the tying well. A notable
prawn imitation is the
Esmond Drury-designed
General Practitioner.

1 *Crevette Grise* – *France*. A comparison with feather-tied prawn/shrimp imitations. Illustrates the scope of "modern" materials, rather than fur and feather. Latex, as mentioned, may also be used in prawns/shrimps.

2 *Crevette Rose* – *France*. Tail whiskers on this and the preceding pattern have been reduced to half their length in order to fit the page.

3 *Orange Parson* – *UK*. One of the "whole feather" patterns, with overlay of married strands.

4 *Vi-Menn Flua* – *Norway*. Also tied as trout and sea-trout pattern.

5 *Torrish* – *UK*. Also tied with red components where

usually yellow. Both patterns thought to resemble shrimp. Similar is Red Sandy. The pale Torrish is also called the Salscraggie.

6 *Pink-Brown* – *Norway*. Kingsmill Moore theorized that the longer salmon are in the river and the staler they are, the more effective are the orange, through red and claret flies, progressively. UK standards list few red flies, the Kate an exception – more modern dressings include some, mostly unnamed except by descriptions.

1 Sarah (Red) – *Norway*.
Scandinavia has adopted
"eyed" flies for salmon, sea-
trout and trout. Marabou
wing.
2 Golden Demon – *USA*.
Similar to steelhead patterns
of same name. Sometimes
brown squirrel hair is included
in the wing.
3 Chilimps – *Denmark*. Trout
pattern used also for salmon.
"Eyes" are often included.
Wide range of colours within
this style.
4 Durham Ranger – *UK/
general*. Also Silver Ranger,
Black Ranger and Blue
Ranger, with body dressing
altered according to
designation. Sometimes jungle
cock sides as well.

5 Le Ny Faisan – *France*.
Another François Le Ny
pattern from Brittany.
6 Durham Ranger – *UK*.
West Country version,
simplified and more sombre.
7 Ottesen – *Norway*.
Intricacies of traditional
dressing style portrayed.
Scandinavia carries the legacy
of UK styles, as the sport
fishing in its countries was
initially developed by the
landed and leisured English
and Scottish upper classes,
and fly tying tradition was
brought with them.

1 *Popham* – *UK*. Fully
dressed tying with original
ingredients in full, tied in 1901
for Major Traherne's selection
for the Badminton Library.
Francis Francis recommended
it for Scottish Ness and Brora.
2 *Jock Scott* – *UK/general*.
Modern style of dressing the
original pattern. Tied
generously like this presents a
hard silhouette. This is one
style, one interpretation of a
standard pattern. There is a
proliferation of Jocks – Blue,
Purple and Claret – with the
anterior half of the body and
its palmer hackle
corresponding with the
designated colour.
3 *Defeo Nymph* (Scott) –
USA. Included among Lee

Wulff's patterns. A more
realistic silhouette to a salmon
fly. The style is continued in a
series – silver, brown and grey.
The black/yellow of this
pattern reflects the body style
akin to that of the ***Jock
Scott***.
4 *Hair-winged Jock Scott* –
UK/general. Yellow/black
body, bright wing overlaid
with sombre wing and sides is
what is generally acceptable
nowadays.
5 *Jock Scott* – *Scotland/UK/
general*. Tied on original
Pryce-Tannatt Rational long
shank iron, with the emphasis
on slender translucency. This
is as "fully dressed" as the
pattern above, but is less
blocky.

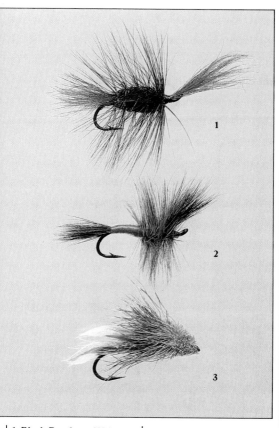

1 Black Bomber – *USA/
Canada*. The Bomber series
took off on the Miramichi in
1967. They have been used
regularly by Geoffrey Hopton
and others in their dry fly
experiments on the Aberdeen
Dee. The touch of red helps
visibility for the angler in
conditions of difficult light
and peat-tinged water.

2 Black Wulff – *USA/Canada*.
A better known pattern, tied
up to 2½ inches in hackle
diameter, and down to the
smallest regular trout sizes.

3 Muddler Minnow – *USA/
general*. This exceptionally
versatile fly design may be
fished either as a dead-drift
dry floater or twitched
slightly, or fished sunk, or

treated as if tied on with a
riffling hitch.

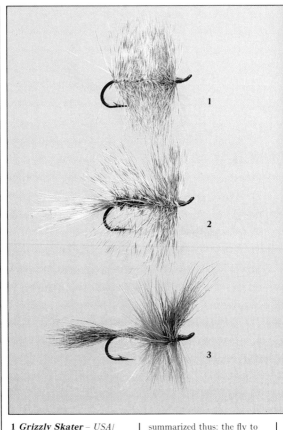

1 *Grizzly Skater* – *USA/Canada*. The way to make this pattern skip and walk over the water, as designed by E. R. Hewitt, is to tie with the curvature of the posterior hackles curling forwards, and that of the anterior hackles curling backwards. This strengthens the hackle tips.

2 *Colonel Monell* – *USA/Canada*. The other early protagonist of the dry fly for salmon, and who wrote about it, was George LaBranche. He credits Colonel Ambrose Monell with taking the first salmon on a dry fly. The river they both favoured was the Upsalquitch in New Brunswick. The method of the early patterns can be summarized thus: the fly to float high; the fly to be placed close to the fish; drag to be avoided. This pattern was Colonel Monell's favourite.

3 *Gray Wulff* – *USA/Canada*. This is probably the most widely used of the Wulff patterns. It is also listed under the trout and sea-trout/steelhead sections, to emphasize its range and utility. It is tied in a wide range of sizes as well.

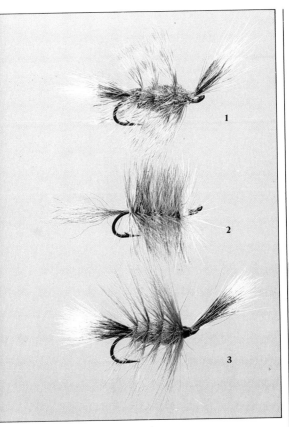

1 *Gray Bomber* – *USA/Canada*. Natural undyed cock hackles are recommended for their stiffness. Caribou hair is one of the best for making the body.

2 *Gray Bivisible* – *USA/Canada*. This is designed to ride high on its hackle tips. The white shoulder hackle aids visibility. There are also other colours of Bivisible, including Black, Brown, etc. The hackle must be tied at right angles to the body, or slanting forwards. Under no circumstances should it slope towards the tail, if good floating is to result.

3 *Brown Bomber* – *USA/Canada*. As an alternative, brown squirrel hair could be tied in for the tail and the forward wing. If the palmer hackle is doubled – two hackles – the fly will stand on its hackle points for the first few casts. (Not to be confused with many other flies designated Brown Bomber in both the USA and UK.)

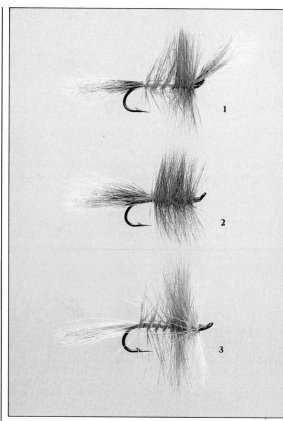

1 Whiskers – *USA/Canada.*
On some occasions a
"twitched" dry fly attracts a
rise while a dead-drift float
does not. The fly should walk
on its hackle points. The
forward wing helps the
balance. In this style there is a
wide variety of natural colour
patterns.

2 McIntosh – *USA/Canada.*
This involves the use of a good
bunch of squirrel hair for a
tail, to ensure high riding
balance. Introduced on the
Margaree by the guide
McIntosh from St Anne's
River.

3 Pink Lady Palmer – *USA/
Canada.* An early pattern
listed with favour by George
LaBranche. His quartet was

Colonel Monell, **Soldier
Palmer** (*see* under Sea-trout/
Steelhead), Mole Palmer, and
this fly. He did not rate any
one better than any other but
justified a variety of patterns
in order to offer a change in
both pattern and size.

1 Sofa Pillow – *USA/Canada*.
This is a stonefly
representation. Lee Wulff
designed a Surface Stone, with
patented plastic body, but a
yellow tube (from electrical
wiring) with the treble
connected through a hole
halfway down the wall of the
tube, produces a similar effect.
The wing is hen pheasant, the
hackle is parachute-tied
natural cock hackle with
partridge hackle. It should be
cast sideways because it is
difficult to make it float.
Many Sedge patterns that
float well have taken salmon.
2 Furnace Dapping – *UK/
general*. See sea-trout section
for more detail on dapping. It
is a method that takes salmon

well in lochs and loughs. A
huge variety of natural
coloured and dyed patterns.
3 Brown Wulff – *USA/
Canada*. Given as a contrast in
size to the following pattern.
Very often the larger flies
move the salmon. A change of
size, downwards, and possibly
of pattern too, then makes
them rise with the intention of
taking.
4 Gold-ribbed Hare's Ear –
UK. Even traditional small
trout dry flies will take
salmon. Any of the standard
patterns where there is a
hatch of natural insects and
salmon are seen to rise to
them: i.e., march browns,
particularly on the
Aberdeenshire Dee, etc.

NOTE: All saltwater tyings should be on stainless or other appropriate hooks. And they must be sharp.

1 *Tarpon (deep-water) Cockroach* – USA. Tied in miniature to illustrate the style. It can be tied up to 10 inches long. Use saddle and not neck hackles, for their extra mobility in the water.
2 *Stu Apte Tarpon Fly* – USA. The need was for a fly that would not offer too much wind resistance in casting, and have a good entry. The result was a pattern with something of the characteristics of a shrimp. This tying is with marabou.
3 *Orange & Yellow* – USA.

This is the Apte principle again. (The style has transferred to fresh water in UK trout patterns such as Peter Gathercole's Concord.) Size and depth can matter more than colour on some occasions. The style permits a huge variation.

1 Red & Yellow – *USA*. The nomenclature is descriptive rather than a designation. Chenille, with its apparent bulk and water absorbency, is incorporated into a number of saltwater patterns.

2 Bonefish Special – *USA*. Bonefish are regarded as classic fly fishing quarry fish. Shy, they hunt the shallow water for shrimps or crabs or small bait fish. Many patterns, therefore, have a passing resemblance to shrimps, and many are tied upside down to avoid snagging up. This pattern comes from the Orvis Index of Fly Patterns.

3 Red/Yellow Deceiver – *USA*. Read Lefty Kreh's *Fly Fishing in Saltwater* for details

of his flies, and as one of the best of the saltwater fly-rodding books. Two or three strands of mylar tinsel each side are highly recommended.

4 Yellow & White – *USA*. The thicker the hackle is tied, the slower the fly will sink. This is sometimes necessary in very shallow water.

5 Red & White – *USA*. Until its use was prohibited, white polar bear hair was a prime material where white hair is incorporated.

6 Red/White – *USA*. In the Apte style. With hackle tied at right angles all along the hook shank, the fly will sink slowly.

1 *Red/White Deceiver* – *USA.* Kreh pattern. Tied in all sizes, with dressing simplified as necessary.

2 *Cream Crazy Charlie* – *USA.* Tied inverted. If keel hooks are used it is sometimes a benefit to open up the point a little, but <u>do not</u> offset it.

3 *Brown & White* – *USA.* Could have been tied upside down.

4 *Frankee Belle* – *USA.* A Joe Brooks pattern. The tying was actually originated by the wives of two fishing friends. A traditional pattern for bonefish. Often tied upside down.

5 *Blue Grizzly* – *USA.* Similar to but more muted than the Blue Death Tarpon, which also has the addition of dyed bucktail.

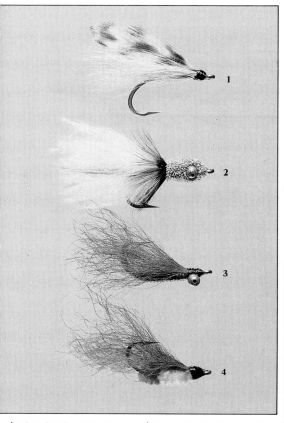

1 Lee Cuddy – *USA*. The Orvis *Index* lists 20 popular saltwater flies. Edson J. Leonard's *Flies* gives many patterns. Kreh's book is useful for its bulk of supporting information on the flies it includes.

2 Permit Fly – *USA*. Tied also with chenille body. A fly for the most frustrating, difficult, unwilling and most coveted of the fly fishing quarries. Bead eyes add weight.

3 Brown Crazy Charlie – *USA*.

4 Brown Snapping Shrimp – *USA*. Also in this style is Grass Shrimp, with light blue Fisttair wing, dyed grizzly hackle tips, and green body;

Golden Mantis Shrimp, golden yellow Fisttair wing with dyed grizzly hackle tips and fluorescent green chenille body.

1 *Tarpon Cockroach* – *USA*.
Collar from natural bucktail.
Plenty of grizzly and natural
dark red game saddle hackles
for the tail in the larger series.
Up to 10 inches. A few strands
of Mylar tinsel. A John
Emery/Norman Duncan
pattern.
2 *Cockroach* – *USA*. Offers
slightly less resistance to the
wind during casting, and
theoretically the tail is less
likely to get tucked out of line
round the hook bend.
3 *Orange Grizzly* – *USA*.
Lighter weight version of the
preceding pattern. As a matter
of practice, every saltwater fly
should be packed ready for use
in a plastic sleeve so as not to
tangle up. When changed, the
discarded pattern should be
washed in fresh water before
being put away even
temporarily.

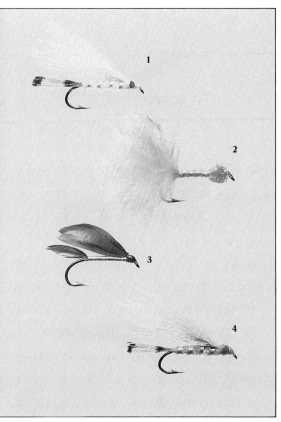

Although many people spin for them, migratory shad will take a fly. The fish are *Alosa sapodissima*, the American shad. The other is *A. mediocris*, the hickory shad, the latter being about half the weight. Basically east coast fish, their introduction to the west coast in 1871 succeeded, so they now have a wide American range. Wet fly is far more effective than dry fly, and most flies are weighted. Beaded patterns are popular, probably because they sink quickly.

1 Chesapeake Bay

2 Shad Dart In the UK, shad run the Severn and Wye: most are caught by spinning rather than by fly fishing. The European species are allis shad (*Alosa alosa*) and twaite shad (*Alosa fallax*), the more common and larger of the two.

3 Connecticut River – *USA*. Still often tied with a glass head.

4 Narraganset Bay – *USA*.

The patterns that follow are about at the extreme end of the craft of fly tying and fly casting on grounds of weight or wind resistance. Special taper lines have been formulated to help cast some of the bass bugs and lures.

1 *Orange Crayfish (Crawdad)* – *USA.* These form quite a part of freshwater fish diet all the world over, if they are available. This tying style is regularly available in Brown and Sandy as well as Orange.

2 *Whit's Softshell Brown Crayfish* – *USA.* The creatures moult. Other patterns include Ted's Crayfish, which is a tying from Theodore J. Godfrey. See Edson J. Leonard's *Flies* for a clipped deerhair pattern. Contrast this with the French salmon ***Crevette*** flies for another possible style interpretation.

3 *Whit's Electric Leech*. Dave Whitlock pattern from the Dan Bailey Catalogue. Includes electric-blue body material. Leeches (*Hirudinea*) are prey to trout or black bass and other fish. There are a number of ways of interpreting them, marabou here forming the tail. Size range seems to be up to 6 inches. Patterns such as ***Woolly Worms*** in their various colours suggest these kinds of creatures.

1 **Black Eelworm** – *USA*.
Also in various colours. Metal
eyes give extra weight.
2 **Black Hair Waterpup** –
USA. Marabou tufts extend
from clipped deerhair body.
3 **Black Chamois Leech** –
USA. Wide range of colours in
this style. The chamois "tail"
is marked with lines of spots
(from an indelible felt-tip pen)
on the colours on which the
spots will stand out. Latex
also has a place in
representing leeches.

The black bass, *Micropterus*, in its six species and four subspecies, and in its successful spread around the world, has been responsible for the development of "bugs". Cork, plastic, wood, foam and clipped deerhair bodies are used, and the patterns may be required to float, to dive, or to form various styles of surface commotion. The range of tyings and styles is vast, so the patterns given are only a small sample. Many patterns are used to good effect for trout.

1 Bumble Bee Diver – *USA*. By cutting the deerhair body at an appropriate angle the fly will dart, during the retrieve. Mixture of marabou, herl and hackle in the tail.

2 Perch Diving Minnow – *USA*. Added strands of flashabou. Note: there should be plenty of clearance at the hook bend, so that the dressing does not spoil the hooking effectiveness.

3 Flat Frog Bug – *USA*. Combination of deerhair colours, plus hackle points tail, and eyes.

1 *Frog Diver* – *USA*. Rubber
appendages, and a different
clip to the deerhair. Weight
may be added, as in some
instances the deerhair gives
bulk rather than buoyancy.
2 *Yellow/Black Bug* – *USA*.
Huge range of colours, and in
varying sequence, in Bug
patterns. Rubber appendages
plus marabou. Other patterns
illustrated suggest more
variations and combinations.
3 *Black Gerruebubble Bug*
– *USA*. This should pop and
splutter along the surface.
Many of the foam, wood or
plastic bodied bugs have
concave heads to enhance the
effect.

1 *Whit's Hair Waterpup* –
USA. Combination of clipped hair body with strip of fur on-the-skin for ringing material/body extension. Newts and salamanders can be imitated as well as the small baitfish.

2 *Hecht Streamer* –
Germany. Truly at the brink of what may be fly-cast. A lure for pike. There is a long tradition of fly-fishing for pike, although only authorities were at variance in their views on how effective a method it was. Many patterns included peacock herl, even entire peacock moons, and some were tied on extended shank trebles for fiercer hooking. Equally many patterns emphasized eyes. Patterns have imitated swallows or sand-martins. Occasionally a fly is tied to imitate waterfowl. A less sophisticated pattern was the tail of a brown calf, furnished with hooks (*Ireland*), no doubt representing a rat. Nowadays big bucktails and streamers are used.

1 Hair Frog – *USA*. A frog style showing use of colour and pattern, through selected tying materials, rather than the greatest attention to shape. The hair "legs" should bend and flex on a retrieve.

2 Wiggle Frog – *USA*. The insertion of springy wire into the legs strengthens the deerhair and permits "kick" as the wire is retrieved. This principle is also used in some crayfish tyings to hold out the claws. Rubber strands have been used for the forefeet.

3 Mouse – *USA/UK/general*. This example has leather ears, leather tail and bead eyes. Simpler versions, merely deerhair cut to approximate shape, are listed in many countries. Trout, bass, pike and atlantic salmon have all been lured by mice, indeed some of the larger trout are unlikely to be caught on smaller flies. Deerhair mice are Charles Brooks' summer standbys for larger trout, but sees a need for them in appropriate imitations of the local voles, meadow mice, whitefooted mice and so on. Cork bodies have also been used, with appropriate covering.

I N D E X

INDEX

INDEX

INDEX